new

Played 38, Won 1
THE WORST TEAMS EVER

Did you spill my pint?
NEIL WARNOCK & TOMMY SMITH SQUARE UP

Futebol, sexo & rock'n'roll
WHY ALL THE BEST GIRLS LOVE JUNINHO

Ryan Giggs
BOOK! OUT AT 21?

ON ACTING,
ITALY &
THE ARSENAL

Yeboah
mighty like a rose

GRAHAM TAYLOR CHRIS ARMSTRONG FRANK SKINNER JIM LEIGHTON THE CASUALS

Conker Editions Ltd
22 Cosby Road
Littlethorpe
Leicester
LE19 2HF
Email: books@conkereditions.co.uk
Website: www.conkereditions.co.uk
First published by Conker Editions Ltd 2021.

A CIP catalogue record for this book is available from the British Library.
13-digit ISBN: 9781999900892
Design and typesetting by Gary Silke.
Printed in the UK by Mixam.

CAN WE NOT KNOCK IT?

A CELEBRATION OF '90s FOOTBALL

SID LAMBERT AND CHRIS SCULL

CONKER

CONTENTS

6

To quote Don Draper in *Mad Men*, "Nostalgia... it's delicate... but potent."

The '90s was inarguably the most important decade in the history of football.

From kung-fu kicks to pop stars missing penalties. From Wenger-inspired dietary revolutions to double sausage and egg McMuffins before training. The decade was a surreal, hilarious melting pot of old worlds colliding with new to create the footballing landscape as we know it today, like two tectonic plates merging as new money and foreign imports flooded into the game. At the same time, rank amateurs were tricking Premier League managers they were related to George Weah to get game time at The Dell.

If I could fire up the DeLorean and go back in time to the 1990s and tell a teenage, football-obsessed young version of me (as he sifted through his huge pile of Ian Pearce Merlin sticker swaps, watched Graeme Le Saux fight his own team-mate David Batty, or sat enraptured every

Saturday night as Le Tissier scored Goal of the Month, month after month) that one day, decades later, those same players would use the bathroom in my windowless East London basement flat, after answering niche questions about their former kit sponsors, you can be sure of two things...

Firstly, it would be a colossal waste of a time machine... Unless, of course, I was also bringing a Wikipedia printout of football results to bet on and change the future, Biff Tannen style. *"Manchester United to score two injury-time goals in the 1999 Champions' League final, you say? I like those odds."*

And secondly, younger me would have laughed at old me like this was some mad, feverish cheese dream: *"You're telling me one day THE Stuart Pearce will stare into my soul with a look of such withering contempt at the fact you forgot the mains power cable for his interview that years later you'll still wake up in a cold sweat at the thought of those psychotic eyes? Get back in your car, grandad, I've got some Championship Manager to be playing..."*

But since nobody has invented time travel yet, the next best thing is here. In your hands.

Within these pages, Chris and Sid have done an incredible job of navigating, harvesting and curating the most interesting and entertaining collection of curiosities and idiosyncrasies from the decade in question. A real treasure trove and literary time machine that serves as a love letter to the most amazing decade in football. One that cannot and never will be repeated, but should be celebrated in all its absurd glory.

I hope you enjoy it as much as I did.

Michael Marden
Quickly Kevin 'director of podcast'

Was football better in the '90s? It's a question we're asked a lot. And the honest answer is 'no'. To watch top-level football these days is to admire the extraordinary athleticism unfolding before your eyes. It's a high-speed hybrid of fast-twitch muscle fibres. Every week we witness goals of the highest calibre, scored by human beings with the lowest body fat percentages that pro sport has to offer.

Was football more fun in the '90s? Unquestionably, yes. To be a football fan these days is to be surrounded by constant noise. The din of the diatribes on every airwave. Forensic analysis of every incident from every angle. And with each microscopic frame, the volume rises. Until it feels like you're surrounded by a take-fuelled tornado of fury.

Sometimes it's easy to look around and ask: *is everyone actually enjoying this?* We are, of course. But it probably wouldn't hurt to sit back every now and then, and not take it all so seriously. Of all the attributes of the late, great Jimmy Greaves, it was his ability to shrug his shoulders and laugh at the glorious chaos of association football that endeared him to us all. After all, it really is *A Funny Old Game*.

This book is a love letter to the laughter of that era. When it was a simpler, gentler time to be a football fan. We rushed home from school to sift through Ceefax for precious updates in 80 words or less. We dialled ClubCall under cover of darkness (stealthily avoiding the bill-payer's permission). And we listened lovingly to the Lightning Seeds as Dalian Atkinson dominated Goal of the Season.

It was a simpler time to be a professional footballer, too. There are doubtless ex-pros out there who would love the wages of the modern player, though not necessarily the workload. The only way the likes of Micky Quinn and Neil Ruddock would have reached 5% body fat would be if they were 95% Heineken. And imagine asking goalhangers like Gary Lineker or Pippo Inzaghi, who only ever left the penalty area due to contractual obligation, to do 90 minutes of high-press defensive duty. That barely leaves any time for having a poo on the pitch or scoring a tap-in.

In these pages you'll find a celebration of the decade in all its glory. And we're confident it's unlike any book you've ever read before, with chapters devoted to cult heroes from yesteryear. For every Cantona, there's a Kevin Francis. For every

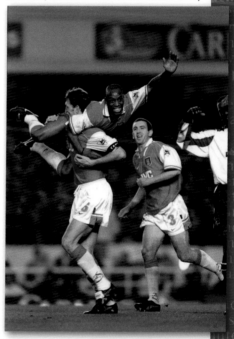

Klinsmann there's a Carl Leaburn. And for every Bergkamp, there's Alan Cork's beard.

We hope you love, love it as much as we loved writing it.

Sid and Chris

INTRODUCTION

9

In November 1996 Southampton were struggling on two fronts. Firstly, they were absolutely hopeless, drifting towards the bottom of the Premier League after a 7-1 thrashing by Everton.

Secondly, they were in the midst of an injury crisis. And with a home fixture against Leeds United on the horizon, manager Graeme Souness was desperate for inspiration.

Thankfully, he received it in the form of a telephone call from George Weah. You know, THE George Weah. The AC Milan striker was tearing up Serie A and widely recognised as the best striker on the planet. He was also a close pal of Souness.

Well, they were close pals in the same way I was close pals with Pamela Anderson during her *Baywatch* years. We'd never actually met, or spoken, but I'd certainly admired her career greatly from afar. And would have jumped at the chance to have any kind of physical/spiritual contact with her whatsoever.

Anyway, not only was the best player in the world calling to give Graeme a pep talk, he also had the answer to his prayers: a striker who could solve all his goalscoring problems.

Ali Dia was a Senegalese international with the highly respectable record of six goals from 15 appearances. Plus, he was available on a free and Southampton could get to the front of the sizeable queue for his services – if Graeme acted fast. It's incredible how haste can affect the human mind. Somehow ignoring the gaping plot holes in the story, Souness went and invited him for a trial the following day. I suppose that's what you do when your only other forward is Gordon Watson.

On the Friday morning before the Leeds game, Dia arrived at Southampton's training ground, whilst Souness proudly confirmed his arrival to the press:

"He's played with George Weah at Paris Saint-Germain, and last year he was playing in the second division in Germany. We've said, come down and train with us for a week or so and see what's what... When someone like that gives you a recommendation, you tend to sit up and take notice."

And that's where the problems started. Because none of those things were true. Dia was not a Senegalese international, had never played at PSG, and if he was in

10

the Bundesliga 2 the previous season, it was only because he'd bought a ticket.

Ali Dia was, in fact, a con man. And a ballsy one at that. He'd been trying this grift the length and breadth of the football pyramid. He'd been rejected by the likes of Port Vale and Gillingham – "We gave the lad a trial, but he was rubbish," said Gills boss Tony Pulis – but that hadn't deterred him. Now here he was, in the top tier of English football.

Dia's performance that day in training at

> ## For all of Dia's theatrics, he couldn't hide one key part of the story: he was a terrible footballer.

Southampton was by all accounts dreadful, though not bad enough to stop Souness naming him on the bench for Leeds.

If that wasn't enough, Southampton's best player, Matt Le Tissier, pulled up with an injury in the first half and had to be substituted. Despite all evidence to contrary, Souness decided best choice to replace the club legend... was Ali Dia.

A man who had never played professional full-time football, had rung up a Premier League manager, pretended to be the best footballer on the planet and recommended himself as new signing, was now Southampton's best

hope of securing three precious points. Extraordinary.

Sadly, there was to be no fairytale finish to this remarkable act of fiction. Because for all of Dia's convincing theatrics, he couldn't hide one key part of the story: he was a terrible footballer.

"He ran around the pitch like Bambi on ice," said Le Tissier in a later interview with *The Guardian*. "It was very, very embarrassing to watch. We were like: 'What's this geezer doing? He's hopeless.' Graeme named him as a sub and we couldn't believe it. I got injured after 20 minutes and when I saw him warming up, I'm going: 'Surely not?' Graeme put him on and he was f**king hopeless, so he took him off again. It was crazy."

His Premier League career lasted 53 minutes. And he was replaced by Ken Monkou. Let's be honest, there are plenty of us reading this who'd be delighted to put that on our gravestones.

In the lead-up to France 98, everything had been going so well. Whisper it quietly, but England were actually quite a good football team.

Having taken the reins from Terry Venables after the euphoria of Euro 96, new boss Glenn Hoddle had moulded the Three Lions into a very capable outfit at international level.

His side had qualified courtesy of a heroic night in Rome when Paul Gascoigne rolled back the years, Paul Ince bled like Terry Butcher in his prime, and Christian Vieri produced the sort of miss that helps Ronny Rosenthal sleep better at night.

That performance left England fans daring to dream all over again. Skinner and Baddiel were getting the band back together and there seemed the very real possibility that after thirty (-two) years of hurt, we might be reunited with the Jules Rimet Trophy.

That dream soon became a nightmare when the World Cup draw was made. It wasn't the opponents that caused the consternation. After all, a group consisting of Tunisia, Romania and Colombia didn't seem too tricky. In fact, Glenn Hoddle was so confident of success, he dropped England's finest midfielder of his generation (Gazza) and replaced him with a workhorse like Rob Lee.*

No, the problem was the timing. England would play their first fixture against Tunisia bang, smack in the middle of a Monday afternoon. How the hell was anyone going to watch it?

What followed was months of panic and scenario planning. The joy of any summer tournament was getting out your wallchart and planning four weeks of blissful football viewing. The Saturday afternoons, the Wednesday evenings, the cheeky early finish on a Friday to watch

an inconsequential bore draw between Bulgaria and the Czech Republic.

But a match on Monday afternoon? This was a logistical disaster. Losing annual leave for a first-round fixture, when those precious free hours might be required for the latter stages, was not an option. So, we were left with no other choice: we were all

going to have to bunk off.

The consequences of mass absenteeism set pulses racing at the Treasury as our finest fiscal minds assessed the economic catastrophe of an entire nation taking a sickie to watch Darren Anderton play at wing-back.**

By hook or by crook, we found a way to watch the game: shops and offices were closed, trains were cancelled, and your favourite teachers even brought tellies into their classrooms.

An audience of countless millions tuned into the Beeb to watch our first foray on French soil, and it was left to that dapper doyen of broadcasting, Des Lynam, to welcome us to proceedings with a killer opening line: *"Good afternoon, shouldn't you be at work?"*

* It wasn't an easy group. And we definitely should have taken Gazza.
** Hoddle had also dropped David Beckham. He was on a real roll here.

In the early '90s, when the internet was still in its infancy and YouTube was merely a glint in the eye of the information superhighway, tape trading was an essential part of popular culture. At my school the most prized asset was a battered copy of *Under Siege*, which featured *Baywatch* beauty Erika Eleniak bursting topless out of a birthday cake.

Similarly, in the summer of 1996, Harry Redknapp had resorted to VHS in his search for an impressive front pair. The West Ham boss was on the hunt for a strike partner for Tony Cottee, and thought he'd struck gold when he found footage of a lad at Sparta Rotterdam called Marco Boogers.

He paid £800,000 for the tall Dutchman, ignoring the age-old transfer maxim: Never sign anyone based on video, just in case they're shit. Looking back, Redknapp may have dodged a bullet. If Sandra had taped that night's *EastEnders*, the Hammers could have started the season with Pat Butcher up front.

It soon became clear that Boogers wasn't quite the imposing target man that the tapes had suggested. He looked like he'd spent pre-season on hunger strike. What's more, the West Ham medical – presumably undertaken using the latest in Fisher-Price technology – had failed to spot a chronic knee injury. There was no way Boogers was going to cope with the hurly-burly of Premier League football.

Despite his physical limitations, the Dutch striker did make one unforgettable contribution to England's top flight after coming on as substitute at Old Trafford. His command of English wasn't particularly good, and something must have got lost in translation as Harry Redknapp gave him his tactical instructions. Boogers mistook the traditional "go out and make a nuisance of yourself" for "go out and cripple Gary Neville," as he launched into a wild two-footed tackle on England's resident right-back mere seconds after entering the fray. He was immediately red-carded and could probably count himself lucky he wasn't spending his winter in Broadmoor.

In the *Match of the Day* studio, Alan Hansen allowed himself a sly grin. A few days earlier the Scot had proclaimed that United would "never win anything with kids" after their opening-day defeat to Aston Villa.

On this evidence, he was probably right. It was going to be hard to win the title if

MARCO BOOGERS

you'd had your foot amputated.

That was Boogers' only memorable contribution in Claret and Blue, though another misunderstanding would taint his reputation in English football. After being signed off with stress, he was then granted compassionate leave to return to his native Holland for the birth of his first child.

He wouldn't be allowed to go quietly. A confused conversation between West Ham's ClubCall reporter, who said the family had travelled "by car again", and a tabloid journalist spawned the infamous headline: BARMY BOOGERS GONE TO LIVE IN A CARAVAN!

> **Boogers mistook the traditional 'go out and make a nuisance of yourself' for 'go out and cripple Gary Neville' as he launched into a wild two-footed tackle on England's resident right-back.**

Now, a quick fact-check would have uncovered that: i) Boogers was neither deemed medically unstable; nor ii) seeking solace from his problems in the simplistic luxury of a recreational vehicle. However, the boys of the British press have never been ones to let facts get in the way of a good story.

Thankfully, Boogers did find his feet again in Holland, becoming something of a club legend at lower-league FC Dordrecht. Yet his legacy on these shores remains one of the most appalling tackles in history, a comical headline and being regularly cited as one of the worst signings in Premier League history.

Kevin Keegan. You remember him. Newcastle United. The Entertainers. "I'd love it if we beat them."

By the mid '90s there was no one more likeable in the football world than good old Double K. He'd done the impossible – taken the Toon to the top of the League. And he'd done it with a smile on his face and Geordie joy in his heart.

But whilst he bled Black and White, the 'Messiah', as he was known affectionately in the North East, also had a healthy respect for the colour green. Ever since the days when he hot-footed to Hamburg for five times the wage he was earning at Liverpool in the late '70s, Keegan always had an acute sense of his own worth. And rightly so. He'd blazed a trail that no other European Footballer of the Year had done before, and that no one has emulated since. Have you ever heard Karl-Heinz Rummenigge's attempt at 'Head Over Heels in Love'? A shambles.

Anyway, the ad men at Sugar Puffs had done their research. When Keegan's profile peaked again, they knew he was their man.

After all, he would advertise absolutely ANYTHING. Slippers, radios, ice lollies, the Green Cross Code – back in the day, if you had the dough, King Kev would show. He'd even starred in a Brut advert with Henry Cooper which reached levels of homoeroticism that *Top Gun* could only dream of.

With Toon riding high in the League, the stage was set for one of the '90s' most iconic adverts. Picture the scene. Newcastle are at Wembley in the Cup final and the scores are tied. With time running out, Keegan turns to his bench for inspiration and finds it in the shape of a big, shaggy-haired giant. No, not Darren Peacock. He'd played from the start.

Keegan decided it was time for the golden-maned Honey Monster himself. No, not Barry Venison. He'd played from the start. Anyway, the big fella did the business, notching the winner and lifting the trophy while Double K was left holding a box of cereal.

It was a fairytale finish, at least until the following season when Sugar Puffs featured Honey Monster playing in goal for Manchester United to reclaim the silverware. Typical Alex Ferguson, always one step ahead.

L ong before *Peaky Blinders* ushered in a renaissance that has already proven itself a tad annoying, the '90s saw only two types of people donning flat caps; farmers and football managers. My evidence for that first category of folk is admittedly drawn exclusively from my only exposure to farmers in the '90s, ie the cult classic film about an orphan pig, *Babe* (in fact, I now realise that the farmer in that film, Arthur Hoggett, bears an uncanny resemblance, flat cap or otherwise, to Jack Charlton).

But anyway, once upon a time flat caps were everywhere in the Premier League and that realisation now, looking back, is absolutely absurd. In the modern era, Tony Pulis and Jurgen Klopp have popularised, and led to an acceptance of, the baseball-capped manager marauding the technical area; but it really feels now that baseball caps are the absolute limit of hat fashion for the modern manager.

On the hat spectrum, you've got baseball caps and beanies at the acceptable end, and everything to the right of that – the fedora, the panama, trilby, bowler and, indeed, the flat cap – make too much of a statement to be acceptable.

Yet despite this, a trail was blazed back in the '90s by the likes of the following flat-cap legends.

Frank Burrows

Across managerial spells at Cardiff, Portsmouth and Swansea, Burrows combined the flat cap with an enormous, bushy moustache which, for me, lends the flat-cap look a far more rural tinge. And to be fair to Frank, of all the managers to wear the flat cap in the '90s, I feel he pulled it off best.

Alan Ball

However, Alan 'Bally' Ball would combine the flat cap with a worn-out tracksuit top; the whole effort never really seemed to mesh together. Frank Burrows could pull off the flat cap and look like landed gentry.

> *Burrows combined the flat cap with an enormous, bushy moustache which, for me, lends the flat-cap look a far more rural tinge.*

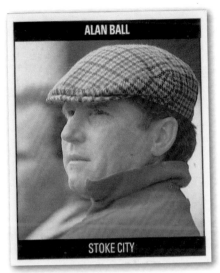

ALAN BALL

STOKE CITY

In comparison, the itinerant Stoke/Saints/City boss looked like a renegade farmhand who might be caught on CCTV, fly-tipping down some country lane.

Jack Charlton

But nowhere was the flat cap more out of place than on the international stage, where Jack Charlton ploughed on with the look as Ireland manager.

> ❝ *Alan 'Bally' Ball looked like a renegade farmhand who might be caught on CCTV, fly-tipping down some country lane.* ❞

In Jack's defence, Ireland is far more agricultural so I can see how this look may have been inspired by his surroundings. And then there was all that hunting, shooting and fishing that he got up to on the

telly. Having a famous footballer roaming the countryside in a flat cap with a rod and shotgun gave rise to one of the great pun-based TV titles... *Jack's Game*.

Sadly though, as far as I can see from my research, Jack never debuted the flat cap at a World Cup; he was hatless at Italia 90 and donned that classic white baseball cap for USA 94 (which was certainly the right decision, given how much the soaring temperatures would have been accentuated by a heavy, woollen headpiece).

In recent years, Pep Guardiola has experimented on a couple of occasions with the flat cap, but not to any regular extent. Perhaps our only hope of the flat cap becoming, once again, a regular occurence in Premier League dugouts would be a rebooting of the *Babe* franchise?

"That'll do Pep, that'll do..."

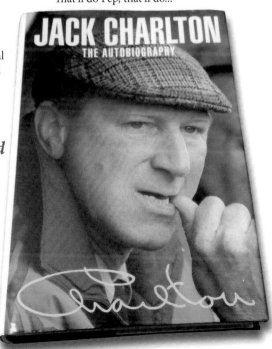

JACK CHARLTON
THE AUTOBIOGRAPHY

By October 1993 Graham Taylor's first – and only – World Cup qualifying campaign as England boss had flirted constantly with disaster. His insistence on dropping good players, picking crap ones and then playing them out of position had yielded a series of dreadful results. The nadir was a 2-0 defeat in Norway where England fans sang "We're so bad, it's unbelievable" whilst watching Carlton Palmer in central midfield.

Yet somehow, thanks to results elsewhere, they travelled to Rotterdam needing only a draw with Holland to earn themselves a qualifying spot for USA 94.

In the 57th minute, it seemed an unlikely victory was on the cards. David Platt broke Holland's offside trap and charged past Ronald Koeman, through on goal. The ageing Dutchman had no choice. A tug on the shirt. A foul. A linesman's flag. And shortly, a penalty and a red card.

To the disbelief of the whole stadium, referee Karl-Josef Assenmacher opted against both. You could argue that the initial contact was outside the box, but in the realms of catastrophic human decision-making, not giving Koeman a red

card is up there with Katie Price's music career. Entirely un-f**king-justifiable.

On the touchline, the England bench raged, with Taylor taking out his frustrations on the fourth assistant before eventually placing a calm hand around the linesman to lament, "I was just saying to your colleague, the referee's got me the sack. Thank him ever so much for that, won't you?"

Ever the gentleman right up to the bitter end, Taylor was partly right. Though it wasn't the bloke with the whistle who played Gary Pallister at wing-back in Oslo.

With staff and players still seething, the Dutch went down the pitch and won a free-kick in dangerous territory. Up stepped Koeman, only for Tony Dorigo to make a heroic block and save the day. Assenmacher, concerned that he hadn't done quite enough to gift the Oranje victory, ordered it to be re-taken for encroachment.

A study of the census reveals that there were 48 million people living in England at the time. And all but one could see what Koeman was going to do with his second attempt. Sadly, that individual was playing

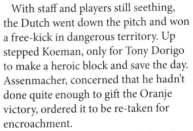

> **Taylor's insistence on dropping good players, picking crap ones and then playing them out of position had yielded a series of dreadful results.**

in goal for the national team. As ITV commentator Brian Moore screamed, "He's going to clip one!" David Seaman stayed rooted to the spot. The ball went in the net and England were all but eliminated. A late strike from Dennis Bergkamp sealed their fate. And Taylor's, too. The following game against San Marino would be his last.

As for Koeman, he even made an appearance on *Fantasy Football League*'s 'Phoenix from the Flames', where he recreated that professional foul against a backdrop of gags about Willie Thorne, the Milky Bar Kid and Victor Meldrew (in hindsight, it's somewhat surprising that at least one of those three didn't get a call-up during Taylor's reign).

It's a good sketch, but for those who remember England in the '90s, Koeman's name provokes about as much mirth as the Poll Tax.

By the summer of 1996 West Ham boss Harry Redknapp had developed a reputation as a shrewd operator in the transfer market. He'd brought back fan favourites Tony Cottee and Julian Dicks on cut-price deals and signed Slaven Bilic for peanuts from Karlsruhe.

The next deal would be his most outrageous yet. Portuguese legend Paulo Futre, one of the best number tens in football history, was on his way to Blighty to wear Claret and Blue.

He arrived for his first day at training in a limo, and showed enough of the old razzle-dazzle to convince Redknapp that he was ready for action. His eagerly waited debut would be at Arsenal on the opening day of the season.

Above ground, thousands of Hammers had amassed in the away end, anxiously awaiting sight of one of the most famous footballers of his generation.

Meanwhile, deep in the bowels of Highbury, a colossal shitstorm was brewing. Before a ball had even been kicked, West Ham were dealing with their first crisis of the 1996/97 season.

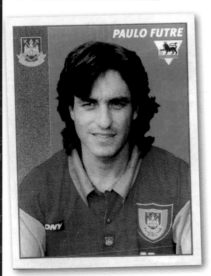

PAULO FUTRE

Paulo Futre, the Portuguese genius, was refusing to play.

Whilst all the players around him were preparing themselves for the big kick-off, Harry Redknapp was trying to shield kitman Eddie Gillam from Futre's rage. His crime? He'd handed Paulo a shirt with the number 16 on it. Short of defecating on his ancestors' graves, Futre could not comprehend a greater insult. One of the world's most gifted players, a European Cup winner, the man dubbed 'The Portuguese Maradona', a footballing sensation who had played for the likes of Porto, Atletico Madrid and AC Milan, was being denied his rightful shirt... because of John Moncur?

> ❝ *Thousands of Hammers had amassed in the away end, anxiously awaiting sight of one of the most famous footballers of his generation.*

Harry did his best to mediate. After all, the shirts had been printed and thousands of Hammers' fans were proudly sporting FUTRE 16 in the away end. Couldn't they sort it out later, old son?

F**k you. I no play.

Futre would not be calmed. He changed back into his civvies and headed for the car park. Which left Harry with an even bigger problem. The teams had been submitted to the referee and, by law, no changes could be made. Futre, now halfway to his hotel, was due on the pitch in a matter of minutes. West Ham would have to start the season with ten men, unless their gaffer could muster up some magic.

The Hammers boss marched into the

referee's office and did the decent thing: he blamed it on his assistant, Frank Lampard Senior. Dear old Frank, never the best of spellers, had forgotten his glasses. He'd meant to write down Stevie Jones, the workhorse forward signed from Billericay, and scribbled the name of Portugal's greatest footballer instead.

It was an honest mistake. Could have happened to anyone, Ref.

The official accepted the unlikely excuse. After all, we all make mistakes. Thankfully, West Ham started the game with eleven players, who duly rolled over and lost 2-0.

Damage limitation began the following week when Futre appeared, his legal team in tow, to convince the club to transfer ownership of the shirt. Moncur was hardly a student of the law. The closest he got to the finer points of courtroom etiquette was watching re-runs of *Perry Mason* after training. However, the madcap midfielder knew a good deal when he saw it. Futre offered a six-figure sum and two weeks in his private villa in the Algarve. Case closed. The shirt crisis had reached an expensive conclusion.

> **Meanwhile, deep in the bowels of Highbury, a colossal shitstorm was brewing.**

And so too did Futre's Claret and Blue career, soon after. In hindsight, how the veteran ever passed his medical at Chadwell Heath will remain one of the game's great mysteries. Evidently, West Ham's outdated, broken, bargain-basement X-ray equipment failed to spot the gaping holes in both his kneecaps which made his limbs about as structurally sound as a packet of Twiglets.

A few weeks after the high-jinks at

Highbury, Futre was folded like an accordion courtesy of a bruising tackle from Wimbledon's midfield. It was his second – and last – start at Upton Park. The final glimpse the West Ham faithful had of one of the most gifted playmakers of the century was him hobbling off, wearing the grimace of a man who knew his race was run.

There were a couple of feeble attempts to come back in Spain and Japan, but the game was up on that sunny afternoon in September when his last start at any meaningful level of football had seen him upstaged by Efan Ekoku.

Still, at least he had the right shirt on.

You don't tug on Superman's cape. You don't pull the mask off the Lone Ranger. And you certainly don't spit on a German's mullet. On a controversial June night in 1990, Frank Rijkaard entered football's Hall of Shame with an act of spit-flinging shithousing that shocked the world.

We should have expected it, really. Holland and Germany's rivalry was hardly a secret. There were half-hearted attempts at cordiality – a bit like He-Man bumping into Skeletor in the post office – but it didn't take much for the hatred to rise to the surface.

The teams entered the knockout stages of Italia 90 in starkly contrasting form.

The Germans had stormed the group stage, while Holland were no more than mediocre. Their famous threesome of Gullit, Rijkaard and Van Basten were woefully out of sorts. It's sometimes like that with a trio. It only takes one member to lose their mojo and the whole thing falls to pieces. Just ask Bros.

Against the Germans it was Rijkaard that let the side down. It started when a crude tackle on Voller earned him a deserved booking. Initially, the Dutchman displayed the sort of incredulity Harry Redknapp reserves for the taxman. Then he lost his mind completely.

With the referee's back turned, Rijkaard deposited a sly dollop of spittle on the

German's hair as he ran past. The tightness of Voller's curls caused a crucial time delay between the moment of impact and him registering the missile. By the time he complained to the official, it was too late. He too was booked. Presumably for being a pain in the arse.

Tempers frayed again moments later. A melee in the Dutch goalmouth, in which Voller was clearly the injured party, saw both men sent off. The Marseille man was incredulous. Just for good measure Rijkaard gobbed at him again as they departed. This time the mid-air mucus was captured in glorious slo-mo as it landed on Voller's ear.

There was disgust in the TV studios. Sickening. Appalling. Revolting. The ITV pundits were pushing their vocabularies to the very limits. Thankfully, Big Jack Charlton was there to restore order. "I'd have chinned him," said the Irish boss.

The incident remains a mainstay of any self-respecting Italia 90 montage. Indeed, despite Voller accepting his apology with good grace, Rijkaard was christened 'The Llama' by an unforgiving German press.

The irony is that, until this time, the act of spitting amongst the impressionable youth of Great Britain was anything but repulsive. It was practically an Olympic sport, practiced feverishly the length and breadth of the land. Bored kids, with no technology at their disposal, would routinely line up and take their turn to see whose gob could cover most distance in the pressure-cooker situation of the school playground. Winning was like a badge of honour and that acclaim would follow you wherever you went: "That's Colin. He once gobbed over an entire hopscotch."

Now that was gone. Spitting was officially a despicable act. Rijkaard had not only ruined football's reputation. He'd robbed a generation of their hard-earned fame.

MET *Echte Boter* KRIJG JE ZE WEER AAN TAFEL.

Epilogue: Things Can Only Get Butter
They say time is a great healer. In football, it's TV adverts. Graham Taylor mocked his own catchphrase for Yellow Pages, Gareth Southgate exorcised the ghosts of Euro 96 for Pizza Hut.

If anything could heal the divide between Voller and Rijkaard, we should have known it would be advertising. In 1996, when the marketing men at Echte Butter brainstormed their next campaign they weren't just worried about sales and ad spend, they also wanted to make a humanitarian gesture by righting one of football's great wrongs.

That's how it came to be that the two adversaries were pictured in matching cream robes, sharing slices of toast on a resplendent spring morning. The image was captioned "Everything in butter again", a reference to an old German proverb that sounds distinctly like one of Ainsley Harriott's brand pillars. The protagonists both donated their fees to charity, and the hatchet was well and truly buried.

There was lots of kicking. And running. And their best player accidentally had a poo on the pitch. As introductions to major tournaments go, England's efforts at Italia 90 were about as uninspiring as it gets.

In the build-up to the much-anticipated opener against the Republic of Ireland, the TV viewers back home had well and truly caught World Cup fever. The exotic settings, the kaleidoscopic crowds and the haunting tones of 'Nessun Dorma' had made Italia 90 essential viewing.

For Gary Lineker, England's talismanic goalhanger supreme and the man on a mission to topple Bobby Charlton's international scoring record, the tournament was a chance at redemption. Two years earlier he'd contracted hepatitis ahead of the European Championships and been little more than a passenger as the Three Lions went home with their tails between their legs after being mauled by Ireland, Holland and the USSR.

Things started to go awry with the prior evening's pre-match pasta. Never mind the complex carbohydrates, the England striker had more basic needs on his mind. He had to find a khazi. Fast.

Unbeknownst to his team-mates, disaster had struck on the eve of the showpiece. Their top goalscorer had the raging squits.

GIVE ME TWO MINUTES LADS

Despite a fitful night's sleep, when he spent more time on the porcelain than the pillow, Lineker made the decision not to tell Bobby Robson of his unfortunate affliction. So England's number ten soldiered on, despite his chronic need for a number two. He ambled through the warm-up with a sense of quiet dread on his face, aware that the merest hint of muscular movement could provoke mass destruction from his arsehole.

And, incredibly, he managed to score the opening goal of the game. His duty done for Queen and Country, he spent the rest of the half nursing his anus horribilis, praying he could reach half-time and the safe haven of the stadium shitter.

Any aspiration of a more comfortable second half disappeared soon after the restart. Over-stretching in pursuit of another aimless punt downfield, Lineker realised that last night's ravioli had momentarily escaped his ringpiece.

These are the moments when experience counts. Sensing the need to act quickly before the rogue stool escaped from his underwear into his Umbros, Lineker did the sensible thing, collapsing to the floor in apparent agony. The trainer rushed on to the pitch, but soon found himself in a hopeless situation. He had the very latest in medical science at his disposal, but what he needed more urgently was a big stick of Glade Peach Blossom.

Meanwhile, on the ITV broadcast, commentator Brian Moore echoed the concerns of the entire nation about the apparent injury. Could it be muscular? Was it a strain? Had he torn something? Technically, he was right on all three counts, I suppose.

To his credit, Lineker persevered and managed to keep the exact truth about his escaping turd a secret for many years afterwards. And looking back, perhaps this was what solidified his credentials as the heir apparent to the mighty Des Lynam. The moustachioed master of BBC broadcasts was known universally for his unflappable demeanour. Live television is a stressful business, you know. You're often at the mercy of last-minute chaos. The key is to keep your head when all around are losing theirs, which Des did with such aplomb on so many occasions.

However, talents of that order were few and far between. And the BBC bigwigs had to be scenario-planning for the day that Des waved goodbye. There were some entirely respectable options at their disposal. Both Steve Rider and Ray Stubbs

> ## Over-stretching in pursuit of another punt downfield, Lineker realised that last night's ravioli had momentarily escaped his ringpiece.

had proven capable deputies for Des in the *Grandstand* hotseat.

But If Gary Lineker could shit himself on football's biggest stage, in front of a global audience of millions, then surely he'd be alright with a last-minute cancellation of the 14.45 at Aintree?

As for the match itself, a Kevin Sheedy goal levelled for the Irish and the spoils were shared. Afterwards, both managers declared themselves reasonably pleased with the outcome.

However, the world's media weren't so impressed. The football had been utterly dire, the game had been a stinker (in every sense), and Italy's leading newspaper declared the match "an ugly stain" on the World Cup.

If only they'd known.

When the United States was announced as the host for World Cup 94, you just knew there'd be drama. In the build-up to the tournament there was much discussion around how to make 'soccer' more palatable for the largely clueless American TV audience.

There were all sorts of wild and wacky ideas to increase the entertainment, such as bigger nets and more shots on target. If Chief Brody had thought of that, he could have saved Amity Island a lot of bloodshed.

In the event, the rules stayed mostly intact and the competition delivered drama from the outset, including a controversial penalty incident in the opening ceremony. There seemed little contact on Diana Ross as she belted out a medley of her greatest hits whilst bursting through the line of cheerleaders. Though pundits might argue that any time you pack the penalty area with schoolchildren dressed as satellite dishes (a nod to the might of America's cable networks) you're inviting the striker to make the most of it.

USA — DIANA ROSS

The platinum-selling songstress got to her feet and readied herself for the spot-kick. Despite her relative inexperience in these scenarios, she employed the rarely seen stuttering run-up. In England, only John Aldridge did the same. But he wasn't wearing heels. It proved a fatal flaw as Ross spooned her effort well wide of the target.

> *Ross employed the rarely seen stuttering run-up. In England, only John Aldridge did the same. But he wasn't wearing heels.*

Some said justice was done. Others felt Motown's most successful artist was hard done by. There's enough pressure taking a penalty at the World Cup, without having to remember the lyrics for 'I'm Coming Out' at the same time.

Worse was yet to come. In a classic case of picking players on reputation rather than form, the creative director for the ceremony had made a catastrophic misjudgement of Ross's ability. Clearly expecting some sort of Julian Dicks-style ripsnorter, he'd rigged the goalposts to split in two from the crossbar the moment Ross struck the ball. What followed was a cringeworthy episode as Ross sauntered through the collapsed structure, despite her attempt rolling pitifully towards the corner flag.

The Ross Incident set the tone for an all-action start to America's showpiece, and it would finish in poetic fashion 30 days later when another curly-haired global icon – Roberto Baggio – would also fail miserably from 12 yards.

I guess you could call that a chain reaction.

Early in the 1992/93 season, Paul Warhurst was living a fairly unremarkable career as a professional footballer. After earning England Under-21 caps with Oldham, he'd moved to Sheffield Wednesday and carved out a reputation as a solid, if unspectacular, Premier League central defender.

Wednesday, under the guidance of manager Trevor Francis, were a decent attacking outfit. John Sheridan played champagne passes across the middle of the park, Chris Waddle was still one of the most skilful players in the League, and David Hirst's left foot was capable of extraordinary acts of violence.

Nobody noticed the defence. And certainly nobody noticed Warhurst. In an age where Sky's hullabaloo meant footballers were slowly becoming household names, Wednesday's dependable centre-half was still effectively Mr Nobody.

He'd played 37 games without scoring in his debut season at Hillsborough, whilst his team-mates grabbed all the headlines. Kids in Sheffield were re-enacting Waddle's wing wizardry, or hammering shots like Hirst. There wasn't much playground kudos for quietly ushering a ball out of play like Warhurst.

> **Overnight, Warhurst turned into the most lethal centre-forward in the country.**

Then, in September 1992, an injury crisis left Trevor Francis in desperate need of strikers. Against all odds, he took a punt on Warhurst, hoping his speed would complement Mark Bright's aerial prowess. The makeshift forward notched in his first game, before grabbing three more goals over two legs of the UEFA Cup tie with Spora Luxembourg. This said more about the standard of the opposition than anything else. I'm not saying they were shit, but you could have probably stuck Roy Hattersley up top and fancied him to nick a goal.

When David Hirst returned to fitness, the fun little experiment seemed over. Warhurst happily returned to the anonymity of the back four – until more injuries in January meant Francis came knocking at his door again.

Only this time it was different. Very different.

Overnight, Warhurst turned into the most lethal centre-forward in the country. He embarked on an extraordinary run of 12 goals in 12 games, propelling Wednesday up the League and into two domestic cup finals.

It wasn't just the quantity of goals that was catching the eye. It was the quality. He was tearing past defenders at will, hitting the top corner with both feet, and

SHEFFIELD WEDNESDAY

PAUL WARHURST

powering back-post headers into the net. To put this into modern-day context, it would be like Wolves chucking shot-shy Conor Coady up front and watching him morph into Cristiano Ronaldo.

Even Skynet couldn't manufacture a striker as f**king magnificent as this. He was a machine. He couldn't be reasoned with. He couldn't be bargained with. He didn't feel pity, remorse or fear. And he certainly wasn't going to go back to playing the offside trap with Nigel Pearson.

He was outscoring the likes of Ian Wright, Les Ferdinand and Teddy Sheringham. His incredible form was rewarded with a call-up to Graham Taylor's England squad. Within the space of just three months, he'd gone from jobbing centre-back to a potential England number nine.

His manager didn't quite know what to make of it all. Hardly a risk-taker, was the wily Trevor Francis. He had the air of a man who'd spent a lifetime quietly lobbying for champagne corks to be replaced with ring pulls.

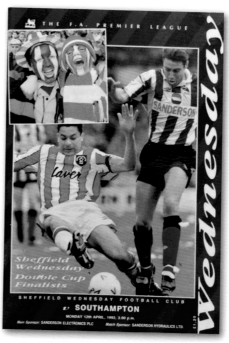

> **Trevor Francis had the air of a man who'd spent a lifetime quietly lobbying for champagne corks to be replaced with ring pulls.**

He was also the genius who had famously rejected Eric Cantona a year earlier when he had the chance to sign the Frenchman on a free transfer. Hindsight makes fools of us all, but it takes a special judge of a player to turn down the most important player in Premier League history because you thought Nigel Jemson would win more flick-ons.

All of which probably explains why Warhurst was jettisoned in favour of David Hirst for the FA Cup final with Arsenal. In fairness to Francis, another injury crisis (training at Sheffield Wednesday in this era seemed more hazardous to your health than enlisting with the SAS) meant they were now short at the back, so he played it safe and pulled his multi-talented star back into defence.

The relationship between player and manager soured. Warhurst moved to Blackburn the following season, but two catastrophic leg breaks meant he never regained that sparkling form of 1993 and he eventually reinvented himself again as a holding midfielder.

Nonetheless, his story was an inspiration to us all. There were still fairytales in football. From unassuming stopper to unstoppable striker. For a few weeks in 1993, Paul Warhurst lived the dream.

The footballing cast of the modern game are all made up of the same basic ingredients: they're athletic, lithe, ripped and quick. Appearance-wise, they all come from the same cookie cutter, being largely one homogenous set of competitors. The only differentiator now is tall or small. But in an age when Lionel Messi is considered 'small' at 5'7", it's worth remembering that the '90s definition included 'Little' Alan Wright, who dominated Villa's left wing at a Ronnie Corbett-esque 5'4".

What's even more remarkable, looking back, is that the professional game didn't merely feature vertically challenged players but the horizontally challenged, too.

Now I don't just refer here to players whose weight absolutely ballooned after retirement (Jamie Pollock, Neil Shipperley and the 'original' Ronaldo to name a few).

There were players who used to go out and play top-level football, for a job, while being substantially overweight.

And this wasn't the result of some curious medical condition. Instead, it had everything to do with a delightful lack of professionalism that some players used to wear like a badge of honour.

Neil Ruddock

One such proponent of this philosophy was former Liverpool and West Ham defender, Neil Ruddock. Stan Collymore has shared the story that upon joining Liverpool in 1995, he was sent to the gym to work on his cardio. Once there, he saw the physio demanding that 'Razor' jump on the treadmill in an effort to shed a few unnecessary pounds. Ruddock took the advice on board, got on the treadmill and fired it up – only to jump off the second the physio left the room. Collymore then witnessed the spectacle of professional footballer Neil Ruddock sitting down on the floor, pulling a newspaper and bacon butty out of his bag and commencing to do the very opposite of losing weight. When the time was right, he tipped a glass of water over his head and jumped back on to the running machine, prompting the physio to comment to the onlooking youth team: "Now that's a proper professional."

Tomas Brolin

By the time Tomas Brolin made his way to Leeds in 1995, he'd won the 1992 Coppa Italia, finished joint top scorer at Euro 92, won the 1993 Cup Winners' Cup and the 1993 UEFA Super Cup. He'd been top scorer for Sweden at USA 94 and won the 1995 UEFA Cup. But there was one prize that eluded him at Elland Road; the award for not being the chubbiest on the pitch at any given time.

Brolin was a disaster for Leeds. After a 5-0 defeat to Liverpool on 20th January 1996, manager Howard Wilkinson popped up on *Match of the Day* to accuse Tomas of "not pulling his weight", which would have been quite the accomplishment had he managed it. Brolin, on £10k a week, would eventually stop turning up for training. This led to a two-year saga whereby Leeds failed hopelessly in trying to offload their £4.5 million signing. As his weight ballooned, so did his negative reputation in

Yorkshire. In 2003, Leeds fans voted him 'the Worst Player in Living Memory', although it's fair to speculate that his reputation among local takeaways was substantially more positive.

As his weight ballooned, so did his negative reputation in Yorkshire.

Neville Southall

But probably the most shining example of the '90s footballing 'larger man' would be Wales and Everton goalkeeper Neville Southall, who inexplicably played with a cat-like nimbleness that belied his considerable belly.

Southall became a legend for the Toffees, from his debut in 1981 right through to his final season in 1998, some 17 years later. He's the most decorated player in Everton's history. But most impressive of all, he did it all with a sizeable weight

disadvantage. He looked so unlike a professional footballer that in the summer of 1995 (weeks after he'd just won the FA Cup) the Queen handed Nev an MBE and enquired, "What will you do, now that you're retired?" For starters, he kept a clean sheet in the Charity Shield a couple of months later.

Neville Southall was absolutely magnificent to watch; his reaction speed boggled the mind. Then there was Mark Bosnich, Gazza, Diego Maradona, Jan Molby, Micky Quinn.

And here's the thing about seeing a big man like that play professional football; it drills home that these are indeed just normal people breathing the same air as the rest of us. Professional footballers now are other-worldly. I have no idea what they do all day, I'm not sure most of us could relate to them. Which is why it was so comforting in the '90s to go to a football ground and see a fat bloke trotting around, giving it a good old go with differing results. It proved that these were, indeed, fallible men, with the same life experiences as you or I. You might see them around town, or most likely, in the pub after a game; you could imagine buying them a drink, and you could imagine them necking it.

And although Howard Wilkinson would no doubt disagree, the rounder footballer of yesteryear is not just missed by catering services within a ten-mile radius of football grounds, it's missed by all football fans who cherished the physical variety of the '90s.

A solid effort in the genre of football on film. It felt like the leading man had an impossible job to play the main protagonist and the film was never going to live up to the heights of the book. Mind you, some people say the same thing about The Bible.

I don't know much about current fashion trends, but as far as I can work out, if Jeff Banks were still doing *The Clothes Show*, it's likely he'd have something to say on the latest garment craze: oversized. But I wonder how many of today's current crop of style icons realise that English football, at all levels, pioneered this look to horrific effect in the mid '90s?

If you look at most football shirts from the 1990/91 season, you will see that they are relatively tailored. The shirt sits on the shoulders, the fabric neatly on the arms, as had been the case for most of fashion history. Then, through 1991 to 1993, you'll notice the shoulders slightly expand.

But come 1993 and we see an influx of kit manufacturers who have presumably never either designed, or seen, a football shirt before. Among the worst offenders are the likes of Pony (West Ham and Southampton), Ribero (Wimbledon, Coventry City and Norwich City) and Clubhouse (QPR). You can understand rookie mistakes made by these entrants, but what's the excuse for the likes of your Adidas, Umbro and Nikes?

Come 1995 and it's almost as if the shirtmakers have completely ignored the fact that these clothes have to be worn by humans, and professional athlete humans at that. The top of the sleeve now starts just above the elbow, AND THE SIZE OF THE SLEEVE! Even Hulk Hogan and his reknowned '24-inch pythons' would have described the fit as loose. The whole shirt was so massive, it was almost the equivalent of playing football in a giant parachute. In an age now where athletic

> *The whole shirt is so massive, it is almost the equivalent of playing football in a giant parachute.*

OFFICIAL 1997
BROCHURE

garments are scientifically engineered to produce peak performance, imagine that not so long ago, football shirts were essentially designed to increase drag.

From 1995-1997, we weren't just playing in enormous shirts, by now the shorts had caught up. I say shorts, they were almost three-quarter-length trousers (or full-size, if you were the legendary pint-sized pop star Prince). It seems every kit manufacturer had somehow lost their mind at the same time.

My beloved West Ham spent two years in the mid '90s in a football kit inspired by our centenary year, and there's a good case for suggesting the kit of 100 years ago may have fit better. We went for a billowing, enormous collar, the points of which almost reached each nipple. Of course, you could always opt to do the collar up with the massive copper buttons mounted on to the shirt.

Manchester United and Liverpool brought equal shame on themselves with their kits in this era. The season after they met in the 1996 FA Cup final, United

released what was surely their droopiest kit in history, swallowing whole the likes of Poborsky, Andy Cole and David May. Liverpool had an effort by Reebok which was arguably even worse, with the 'short-sleeved' home version making its way over Robbie Fowler's wrists, and a cream away kit that somehow managed to be the worst cream-coloured outfit a Liverpool team ever wore in the '90s.

It was an era that literally made no sense. At the time, I don't recall ever questioning the fact that these clothes were getting droopier than Harry Redknapp's eyelids after five non-stop days of watching Marco Boogers on VHS; we all just seemed to accept the fact that football shirts didn't fit any more.

By 1998 it appears the penny finally dropped at the factory that these outfits were indeed football kits not duvet covers, and so the sizes began to shrink – and, by 2000, they actually looked like real clothes again. And so ended the most ill-fitting fashion era of Premier League history.

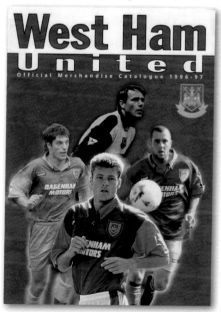

West Ham
United

Official Merchandise Catalogue 1996-97

Imagine, in this day and age, Cristiano Ronaldo's or Lionel Messi's best mate becoming a celebrity by virtue of their close bond and love of both each other and 'the smash'. Visualise for a moment, that fictional best friend having the name 'Javier Six Chins' or 'Pablo Porky Trotters'. You can't, can you? The modern mind can't comprehend it; but in the '90s, just such a phenomenon occurred.

I think it's fair to say few of us will ever have a mate so doggedly loyal, game and true-hearted as Paul Gascoigne's best mate, Jimmy 'Five Bellies' Gardner. They were childhood best friends, Gazza grew up next door to Jimmy's nan. They played football in the street for hours on end and, at some point, the abilities of the natural football genius understandably outstripped those of 'Five Bellies'.

Thereafter, Gazza was headed to the very top of the game and Jimmy, the loyal mate,

> **Their friendship even survived Gazza disassembling Jimmy's mince pie, removing the filling and replacing it with actual cat shit.**

followed just a few steps behind.

The fact their friendship survived the many tests Paul put Jimmy through, is frankly mind-blowing. There was the time at Lazio, as seen in the 1994 TV documentary *Gazza's Italian Diaries*, that our protagonist got up early one morning, dissembled a mince pie, removed the filling and replaced it with actual cat shit.

Having done this, Gazza then wakes Jimmy and asks him if he'd like to start the day with a hot mince pie, which Jimmy of course does. A 30-second blast in the

microwave later, and Gazza is in gleeful hysterics as he tells Jimmy that he's just eaten moggy excrement.

Then there was the time Gazza bet that Jimmy couldn't stand the heat of the flame from a lighter on his septum for five seconds; five seconds later, Jimmy had pocketed £1000.

Or the time Gazza spent thousands of pounds on a state-of-the-art electronic robot, took it home and arranged for it to be programmed to go into Jimmy's room and utter the phrase, "Make a cup of tea, fat man."

On our podcast, Paul Merson shared even more horrific stories. There was the time, down the local boozer, when Gazza offered £100 to Jimmy for maintaining the position of his fingers down one end of a pool table, while Gazza and Merse luzzed the balls from the other. Or Gazza telling Jimmy that he'd give him £1000, but subtract £100 for every dart he hit him with on the walk (or most likely, run) back from the pub.

While there's no doubt that Jimmy had a lot to put up with at times, he certainly led an exciting existence. Not just tagging along for spells at Newcastle, Spurs, Lazio and Rangers but also being in the immediate orbit of the white-hot heat of fame after Italia 90. But arguably best of all were the nights out with Paul, Danny Baker and the flame-haired golden child of the '90s, Chris Evans. An awesome showbiz collection that dominated the tabloids for years.

On one such occasion, Evans splashed out £10k on a bottle of wine for them all; a far cry from the Newcastle Brown Ale Jimmy may well have been chucking back in Gateshead in an alternative dimension.

It's hard now to imagine a famous footballer's best mate sharing the limelight to such an extent.

And speaking of now, a quick look at what Jimmy's been up to since reveals that his weight has dropped from the previous high of 19st, down to a single-belly-sized 13st. In 2010 he successfully ran a half marathon for Sir Bobby Robson's cancer charity (which was presumably a little less stressful without someone following a few paces behind, hoying arrows down your arse crack).

But let the history books record a friendship for the ages, that began playing football in the backstreets of Gateshead and persevered beyond a cat-poo pie.

In 1999, Andy Cole was on top of the world. He'd won the Treble with Manchester United, had scored his 100th Premier League goal, and was back in the England fold under new boss Kevin Keegan. So, he did what any other self-respecting footballer at the peak of his powers would have done.

Did he ask ask for a pay rise? No. Request a transfer to Real Madrid? Of course not. Release an ill-advised R&B single? Abso-f**king-lutely.

'Outstanding' was Cole's debut entry into the UK charts, and he was determined to dress the part. There were no club colours, instead opting for a roll-neck and leather jacket combination that looked like he was auditioning for the part of debt collector in *Lock, Stock*. The lyrics did pay homage to his day job at least, as the striker reaffirmed he was "United forever, whatever the wevver". A dangerous pledge in rainy Manchester.

Still, these comforting words would have been welcomed by legions of Red Devils' fans across the globe, if perhaps diluted somewhat by Andy's subsequent move to Manchester City later in his career.

Anyhow, whilst Cole may not have quite delivered on his promise, the video certainly did. The prolific striker is pictured being driven around the city in an expensive sports car, before arriving at a nightclub where he is unquestionably the guest of honour. In fact, so keen are the hosts to impress their VIP that the dancefloor is cleared to allow an impromptu game of table football. You didn't see that at the Hacienda.

Typically, Cole nets the winner in a frenetic finale against Harchester United's Karl Fletcher (presumably Teddy Sheringham's invite got lost in the post). However, his celebrations were sadly short lived. 'Outstanding' lasted precisely one week in the top 100, peaking at number 68 before disappearing into the black hole of record-store discount bins. It would be easy to poke fun at a music career that saw him trail the likes of Vengaboys and 'Mambo No. 5' in a fairly dismal period for the UK charts. But at least Cole had the courage to try.

And besides, have Lou Bega or Martine McCutcheon ever scored a winner in the dying moments of a Champions' League semi-final in the Stadio delle Alpi? Have they bollocks.

ENHANCED CD
INCLUDES VIDEO

ANDY COLE
OUTSTANDING

AD NAUSEAM

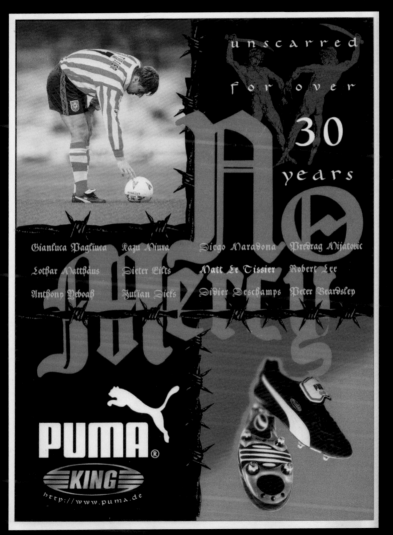

Barbed wire. Naked Romans with big swords. Demonic font. Is this the work of Matt Le Tissier or the Illuminati? Actually, probably best not to ask him that…

Ahead of World Cup 94, our American hosts promised entertainment – and they didn't disappoint. There were goals galore (despite Diana Ross's woes from the penalty spot on opening night), and there were red cards aplenty as referees struggled with Fifa's new criteria for explusion (in some cases, merely stepping on the pitch seemed to put you in danger).

Amidst all the hullablaoo was Bulgaria. Humble Bulgaria, who'd never previously won a game at the World Cup, became unlikely stars of the tournament thanks to a unique mix of players.

The Good: Hristo Stoichkov

Blessed with a left foot like a cannon, the powerful striker had lit up La Liga with his explosive displays for Johan Cruyff's much-heralded 'Dream Team' at Barcelona. But the moody bastard had a reputation as a nightmare to manage. Stoichkov had the sort of temper that made Henry VIII look like The Fonz. Thankfully, in the States he let his feet do the talking by notching six goals.

The Bald(ing): Yordan Letchkov

The unassuming midfielder may have looked like a substitute geography teacher, but beneath his lack of

follicles lay an immense football talent. Unlike the bewigged keeper Bobby Mikhailov, he'd adopted a more pragmatic approach to his sparse scalp. In football terms, he'd played to his strengths: loading the channels, bypassing the midfield and keeping a lone presence up front. Which sounds suspiciously like Tony Pulis's coaching manual.

The Ugly: Trifon Ivanov

Wild-eyed and bearded, the no-nonsense defender remains a routine inclusion on any list of ugliest footballers of the last 30 years. He could boast a visage so utterly terrifying, he'd walk along the beach and the tide would refuse to come in. Rumour had it that Peter Beardsley kept a picture of him in his wallet, pulling it out occasionally when he needed a boost to his self-esteem.

In the tournament itself, this ragtag bunch of journeymen made it all the way to the semis, including a famous win over Germany in the quarter-finals, where Letchkov hit the back of the net with a sublime diving header. Plucky, spunky, big-hearted little Bulgaria had toppled one of football's genuine superpowers. All thanks to that bloke with the bald patch.

HRISTO STOICHKOV
BULGARIA

YORDAN LECHKOV
BULGARIA

TRIFON IVANOV
BULGARIA

niffer. Snaffler. Poacher. There are a
lot of ways to describe goalscorers,
though if you put them on your
LinkedIn profile you might find yourself
on a watchlist for Operation Yewtree.

I've always preferred 'goalhangers'. A
simple term for a simple art. Though when
you were a kid, being labelled as such was
far from complimentary. You were seen as
little more than a glory hunter, capitalising
on others' hard work to steal the spotlight
for yourself. Little did we realise that there
were handsomely paid professionals who
carved entire careers doing exactly that.

The '90s was the last great hurrah for the
Fox in the Box. By the end of the decade,
as tactics developed and systems changed,
it felt like the deck was stacked against
them. It was no longer acceptable for a
professional footballer to hover round
the 18-yard box, scratching his arse and
scuffing one in off his studs. Now you had
to press, run the channels and link up play
to be a worthwhile part of the team.

Yet anyone who knows a goalhanger
knows that teamwork is the last thing on
their mind. It's not about putting a shift
in, or even about your team winning or
losing. All that matters is hitting the net.

And these men were past masters of
their craft.

Gary Lineker

A man who spent nearly his entire career
in the penalty area, Lineker routinely
spent 89 minutes of a football match
living in near-total isolation from the ball.
Playing permanently on the shoulder of
the last man, he would drift right to left
(his Twitter detractors say he spends too
long there these days), doing little of note
before popping up to score the winner.

He started the '90s by scoring four
goals at the World Cup, before bagging
another 50-odd times over the next two

seasons at Tottenham in the old Barclays
First Division. The best thing about
that extraordinary record is that no one
remembers any of them.

You see, Lineker was the absolute master
of scoring rubbish goals. Bucketloads of
them. He's one of the very few strikers
whose highlights looked better on Ceefax.

Micky Quinn

When looking back at the goalgetters of
yesteryear it's easy to get misty-eyed about
the likes of Cantona, Klinsmann and
Solskjaer. But there was once a strange
time when the best striker in England was
a fat Scouser called Mick. And he played
for Coventry City.

Quinn arrived at Highfield Road in 1993,
the wrong side of 30, with a waistline that
looked like he'd spent pre-season locked in
a kebab shop. Nonetheless, the man fondly
labelled 'Sumo' by the Sky Blues' faithful
notched an astonishing ten goals in his
first six Premier League starts.

Despite the billions of pounds of talent that has graced England's top flight since since then, it's a tally that has never looked like being beaten.

> ## Quinn's waistline looked like he had spent pre-season locked in a kebab shop.

Tony Cottee

In 1999/00 Tony Cottee was doing the same thing he'd been doing for the past 17 years: scoring a fair few goals for fairly crap Premier League teams. He'd done it at Everton. He'd done it at West Ham. And now there was he was at Martin O'Neill's Leicester City, 35 years old, feeding off Big Emile Heskey's flick-ons and inexplicably finding himself up amongst the division's top scorers.

Normally, when players have this sort of longevity, there are the usual platitudes to their conditioning and self-discipline. For Cottee, it was more simple: it's hard to get injured if you don't run. Like all great poachers, Cottee preserved his energy for the penalty box. You've got more chance of finding footage of the Loch Ness Monster sharing a pint with Shergar than you have of seeing Cottee score from long range.

Pippo Inzaghi

Famously, when he turned up for his first training session with the national team in 1997, Filippo Inzaghi's performance was so woeful that his team-mates couldn't stop laughing. Not that 'Pippo' was too arsed. He knew his deficiencies: heading, passing and trapping a football, mainly. And besides, he'd heard it all before.

Sir Alex Ferguson said, "That lad was born offside," whilst the great Johan Cruyff was equally sceptical: "He actually can't play football at all." That may be true, but you don't need much technical ability when you're toe-poking the ball 30cm from goal. The rest is all garnish.

Inzaghi's disregard for football's finer points is what makes him so special. He spent the '90s scoring some of the worst goals since records began and celebrating each one like Marco Tardelli on speed. He did it well into the Noughties, too. There's been no one like him since. 'Super Pippo' really was the last of the goalhangers.

FILIPPO INZAGHI

Back in the '90s, some things just went together. Torvill and Dean. Robson and Jerome. Chip and Dale. But for football fans, there are few couplings more evocative than Dalian Atkinson and the Goal of the Month music.

In 1992/93 Atkinson was in his second season with Villa. A teenage prodigy at Ipswich, he'd starred at Sheffield Wednesday before jetting off for a spell with Real Sociedad. Like a dodgy timeshare salesman, he'd had some fun in the Spanish sun and was attempting to rebuild his reputation back home. It didn't take long.

Big Ron partnered the powerhouse with Dean Saunders and soon the pair had propelled Villa into title contention. Then, on a rainy day at Selhurst Park in October, Dalian Atkinson wrote himself into Premier League history.

When the Villa striker picked up the ball barely 30 yards from his own goal, few could have predicted what would happen next. Building momentum like a rhino, Atkinson bulldozed past a powerless Dons midfield. He left Lawrie Sanchez, Gary Elkins (twice) and Scott Fitzgerald in his wake, before uncorking a chip which floated like a crisp packet on the breeze over the flailing Hans Segers.

One of the most iconic goals of the '90s was swiftly followed by one of the most iconic images. These are the moments football supporters long for: the sheer elation of seeing history in the making. Some scream themselves hoarse.

Others grab loved ones, or even total strangers, in delight.

And, occasionally, someone runs on the pitch to hand Dean Saunders an umbrella.

The '90s saw a revolution in the football-hair dichotomy. Whether it was David Beckham's symbiotic relationship with Brylcreem, or Jason McAteer's war on dandruff through Head & Shoulders, the industry's biggest names began to see football as a fertile patch for their advertising spend. However, whilst impressionable youths up and down the land would bowl into Boots looking to bleach their hair like Gazza, there was one hairstyle that stayed on the periphery. The ponytail remained the preserve of the few... and they wore it with pride.

Emmanuel Petit

Very few players can lay claim to winning the English Double and the World Cup whilst sporting the same haircut as My Little Pony. This was a truly glorious mane. And like Sansom (the Biblical one, not Kenny), Petit seemed to derive his strength from it, powering Arsenal's early success under Arsene Wenger. When he played for Chelsea in the early 2000s, he made the unwise decision to chop off the locks and don an alice band instead. He was never the same player again.

Brian Kilcline

In an alternate universe, families of Sasquatch gather round campfires and tell horror stories of Brian Kilcline. The former Coventry, Newcastle and Swindon stopper seemed to defy all norms of personal grooming. He looked the like the sort of man who brushed his teeth and then necked a pint of orange juice. Utterly terrifying.

David Seaman

For years humankind has wondered: "What happens if you merge Tom Selleck's moustache and Steven Seagal's Barnet Fair, with an instinctive shot-stopping ability at football's highest level?"

> *He looked the like the sort of man who brushed his teeth and then necked a pint of orange juice.*

In David Seaman, we finally had our answer. As his reputation grew, so did his hair. In the '90s the Arsenal keeper seemed almost unbeatable, until that fateful day at World Cup 2002 when Ronaldinho lobbed him from 40 yards. One year later, the Brazilian was sporting a ponytail himself. The torch had officially been passed.

Roberto Baggio

Domestic audiences' first glimpse of Baggio came when he danced past the Czech defence and set Italia 90 alight. Throughout the decade, we would enjoy his exploits on *Gazzetta Football Italia*. The club crest would change, though reassuringly his ponytail remained a permanent fixture. By the end of the '90s, 'The Divine Ponytail' had turned from black to grey, and he looked like an ageing wizard – Serie A's answer to Gandalf, always with a Golazzo up his sleeve.

The '90s was the first time fans got a glimpse of football's hallowed ground: the dressing room. Throughout the decade, various camera crews were allowed into the inner sanctums of our top football teams, often with sensational results.

This was long before Netflix's glossy *All Or Nothing* series, which are little more than powder-puff PR pieces. This was meat-and-potatoes football programming, with no creative control, and cameras successfully capturing the reality of football management.

There was no better example than *Premier Passions*, a behind-the-scenes documentary shot during one turbulent Premier League season at Sunderland's Roker Park.

The star of the show was no-nonsense manager Peter Reid, in the midst of a rollercoaster spell in the North East which saw him ultimately take the team from the First Division relegation zone to seventh in the Premier League. Just as in his own playing days, the Gaffer took no prisoners.

Whether he was dishing out a world-class bollocking or driving his team forward, he did it with the most magnificent profanity...

"That's f**king shite. And it's not about f**king tactics and them being great players. It's about f**king arsehole. Which they've got f**king more of on the f**king day."

"I tell you what that is. F**king men against f**king boys all over the f**king park."

"Get your f**king arses in gear. I don't give a f**k about losing, but I tell you what I give a f**k about: losing shite. Not f**king having a go. Not wanting to f**king get up people's arses."

"Get it f**king done. Have the bollocks to get on the f**king ball and pass it."

"If we pass it, we'll beat anyone. I need that belief out there. Because I'm f**king tell you. There's internationals and everything out there. You're as f**king good as them."

"I tell you what. I don't give two f**ks whether we win, lose or draw. But what I want, for 45 minutes, is us getting hold of it all over the f**king pitch."

The advent of Championship Manager pushed the human spirit to hitherto unknown extremes. Sleep was fitful. Food a luxury. Toilet breaks were limited to 12-hour intervals. Which sounds a bit like Terry Waite's memoirs.

However, the gameplay was so wonderfully addictive that we were willing to absorb the toll it took on our minds, bodies and bladders. It was worth it for one more game, one more season, especially when we had these laptop legends at our fingertips.

Nii Lamptey

The Ghanaian was the original Championship Manager 93-94 wonderkid. A diamond hidden in the rough at Anderlecht, who you could pick up for a gratifingly modest fee and shove straight into first-team activity.

Lamptey is part of that elite list of '90s teenagers (Ronaldo, Michael Owen, Doogie Howser) who were thrust into the limelight and performed with admirable aplomb for talent of such tender years.

In an age of kick-and-rush and getting it into the mixer, the Champ Man artificial intelligence was ahead of its time. You simply gave the ball to Lamptey and let his incredible attributes (lightning pace, creativity, flair) do the rest. He was the blueprint for what would later become football's number ten role.

On the actual football pitch, Lamptey wasn't quite the same creative force. Despite his obvious talents he lost his way and spent years wandering football outposts in search of glory. But in our hearts, he'll always be a hero.

NII LAMPTEY

Tommy Svindal Larsen

In the '90s, English football had cottoned on to the fact that Scandinavia was a bargain hunter's dream. And if you were in the market for a classic blood-and-guts midfielder, then Stabaek's Tommy Svindal Larsen was your man.

Bone-crunching tackles, defence-splitting passes, lung-busting sprints from box to box. The Norwegian had it all. Like a Norse warrior of old, he cared little for reputation. It didn't matter whether you were Veron, Beckham, Figo or Zidane. If you got in Tommy's way, you got the treatment. His laptop career was littered with broken bones and silverware aplenty.

In real life, he didn't quite hit the same heights. Though 24 caps for his country shows that the CM scouts weren't too wide of the mark.

Niclas Alexandersson

Long before James Milner made it fashionable, Niclas Alexandersson was the original squad player. Very few in the Champ Man universe have been bestowed

44

with the honour of being equally proficient in defence, midfield or attack.

The Swede was like Polyfilla with peroxide hair. If there was a gap in your team, he filled it. And with the minimum of fuss. 7/10 every week.

Which begged the eternal question: what

was Alexandersson's best position? On the bench, probably. And if you ask fans of Sheffield Wednesday, Everton and West Ham, whom the Swede represented in real life, that sounds about right.

Ibrahima Bakayoko
It was only when we loaded the CD-ROM for Championship Manager 97/98 that we realised the old Pele/Maradona debate had it all wrong. The greatest player to ever walk the Earth was actually a little-known striker playing in Ligue 1.

Ibrahima Bakayoko was essentially a cheat code. A glitch in the Matrix. For any team, in any league, in any country across the globe, the Montpellier forward's signature guaranteed you goals and glory.

Diego's hand may have been blessed by God, but Bakayoko's feet had been created by the universe's most omnipotent force – The Champ Man data editors.

Remember the excitement when it was announced that the Ivorian forward would be joining Everton in October 1998? This was the test of the system. Could the man match the unbridled onward march of the mechanism? If his stats were anywhere near accurate, this would be mankind's biggest advancement in human hybrid technology since RoboCop reported for the afternoon shift in Detroit City.

Unfortunately, a dismal goal return of four goals in 25 games wasn't the kind of statistic we were accustomed to. And he was quickly bombed out of Goodison for a cut-price fee. Turns out he was human, after all.

You're a rookie manager. Your club's broke. And your team's crap. In 1995 things were tough for John Sitton. After a highly respectable career as a pro in the lower leagues, he'd been promoted from youth team boss to joint-manager of Second Division strugglers Leyton Orient. The O's were mired in a relegation battle, on the brink of liquidation, and couldn't afford to pay the players' wages. Short of being Neil Ruddock's dietician, it's hard to imagine a worse job in football.

But Sitton persevered. The TV cameras captured his daily struggles in the incredible fly-on-the-wall documentary, *Orient: Club for a Fiver*. Owner Tony Wood, desperate to sell the club, would have had more chance finding a buyer for a holiday home in Jurassic Park. And with each passing week the pressures grew, until Sitton finally exploded one Saturday afternoon in February. Trailing 1-0 at home to Blackpool, the Gaffer had seen enough – and let rip one of the most iconic team talks of all time:

"That is the f**king straw that broke the camel's back. That is typical f**king Leyton Orient.

You say, 'Sitts, you're too f**king intense, nobody can talk to you. You're this, you're that'. I never f**king followed two good games up with a f**king game like that. The reason I was f**king intense is because I wanted to play well again.

But I'm wasting me breath on some of ya.

F**KING DINNER!

I'm wasting me breath.

What did I say to ya, about good players wanting to be good players all the time? Don't you know how profound that is? Are you not examining the f**king words?

Because you've had two good performances and you think, 'I'm Bertie Big Bollocks, I'll play how I like.'

But you won't play how you like. Because if you play how you like, I'll f**king stick the youth team in. If I'm going to take abuse from a bunch of cockroaches behind me, I'll take abuse by doing it my way.

And that is f**king conformity. Not f**king non-conformity.

So you, you little c**t, when I tell you to do something – and you, you f**king big c**t – when I tell you to do something, do it. And if you come back at me, we'll have a right f**king sort-out in here.

And you can pair up if you like. And you can f**king pick someone else to help you. And you can bring your f**king dinner. Because by the time I'm finished with you, you'll f**king need it. Do you f**king hear what I'm saying or not?"

In an age of Netflix fluff pieces, this remains the gold standard of sports docs, albeit with dire consequences for Sitton. He was fired that season and, despite his reputation as a coach, has never worked in the game since. In reality, such teamtalks are routinely heard in every dressing room in the football pyramid. Unfortunately, this was the only one captured on camera.

It goes to show why football remains so protective of its inner sanctum, desperate to preserve the mystique of managers and players. They want us to believe that it's all about tactics, gegenpressing and sports science. No doubt that plays a part. But make no mistake, when that whistle blows sometimes it's just about big c**ts and little c**ts doing their f**king jobs. John Sitton told us so.

AD NAUSEAM

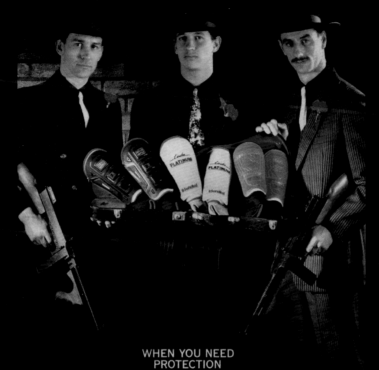

WHEN YOU NEED
PROTECTION

 Seton
Sport & Leisure

"Janice, tell Marketing I've had a great idea. Have you got a pen? Good, because you're going to want to write this down. Listen, we'll get Robbo, Lineker and Rushy dressed up like three c**ts from Bugsy Malone. Guns and everything. Stick 'em next to our shinpads and we'll make a fortune…"

FOREST v. WEST HAM UNITED
Saturday, 26th August, 1995.   Kick-off 3.00 p.m.
Volume 28. Number 2.   Official Match Day Magazine £1.50

In 1995 new Nottingham Forest striker Andrea Silenzi made an entry into the record books by becoming the first – and undoubtedly the worst – Italian to play in the Premier League.

The £1.8 million striker arrived in the East Midlands as a replacement for Liverpool-bound Stan Collymore, whose 22 goals the previous season had propelled Forest to third place. It was an exciting, if rather curious move by gaffer Frank Clark. Replacing a dynamic striker like Collymore with a 6'4" beanpole didn't seem a like-for-like substitution.

Clark was insistent that his new charge was "a typically English centre-forward – strong and powerful, though also good technically." Besides, Silenzi had played at Napoli alongside Careca and Maradona. Just imagine what he could do aided by the likes of Ian Woan and Steve Stone.

Silenzi wasn't the only exotic new arrival from Italy. Dennis Bergkamp had joined Arsenal from Inter Milan, and when the Dutchman experienced some teething troubles adjusting to life in the Premier League, Forest fans' doubts about their new striker were allayed. However, by November Bergkamp had started to find his feet. Meanwhile Silenzi was playing like his shoelaces were tied together.

You're more likely to find footage of Lord Lucan having a pint with Bigfoot than you are any substantial video evidence of Silenzi's Premier League career (three starts, nine substitute appearances and the grand total of zero goals). He is the Sasquatch of the Premier League: a mythical beast who precious few have seen in person, but whose legend remains to this day.

The nadir came during a particularly dire first-half performance in the UEFA Cup which left Alan Hansen fuming. When Gary Lineker pointed out he was an Italian international, the Scot replied: "Were 400 players injured that weekend?"

In fairness, injury had played a part in his downfall. There were rumours he'd arrived with a pre-existing condition that had ruined his last season in Turin. There was also the fact that he had no help settling in to his new environment. In 1995, player liaison was non-existent. The big fella had arrived from Turin, been given an *A-Z*, a copy of *Robin Hood: Prince of Thieves* and then left to fend for himself. *Welcome to Nottingham, son. Now get on with it, you big lump.*

By all accounts the Italian was a throughly nice chap, with a big rep in his homeland, whose physical limitations meant he was essentially crap at football. Given those criteria, Forest fans should be grateful they didn't sign Pavarotti.

The striker left after one season and only scored five more goals in four seasons as a professional. In Italy they still call him 'Il Pennellone', which translates to 'The Big Brush'. Unfortunately, we've not yet found one sizeable enough to wipe the stain of signing Silenzi from Frank Clark's reputation as a manager.

48

England has a rich association with facial hair: WG Grace, opening batsman and Godfather of cricket. Brian Blessed, noted theatricalist and purveyor of good tidings regarding Flash Gordon's health. And, in the early '90s, another unlikely name was added to that list: journeyman striker Alan Cork.

In January 1993 the 33-year-old Sheffield

United forward awoke on the matchday of the FA Cup third-round tie at Burnley and went through his normal pre-match routine: wincing as his joints clicked into action, walking gingerly to the bathroom and staring forlornly into the mirror, wondering whether he could possibly make it through his 16th season as a professional footballer.

Except, on this occasion, he made the fateful decision to eschew tradition and not have a shave until United exited the world's most famous cup competition. The Blades hardly had the richest of cup pedigrees, so at first glance this gambit seemed about as daring a placing a wager on Benny Hill writing a sketch which culminated in him being pursued by a furious gaggle of large-bosomed females.

When Burnley went 2-0 up, Cork was already stroking his chin and preparing to say goodbye to his stubble at 4.45pm. However, the home side promptly scored twice to salvage a draw, and then they went and won the replay. From then on a fairytale was enacted. The Blades progressed through the rounds all the way to the semi-final against arch-rivals Sheffield Wednesday.

By now, Cork's lack of personal grooming had become a media fascination. He looked less and less like a professional athlete, and more like a former tech entrepreneur who'd lost his life savings in an intellectual property lawsuit with Microsoft, and spent the last 20 years drinking himself into a pitiful stupor.

> ## *When Burnley went 2-0 up, Cork was already stroking his chin and preparing to say goodbye to his stubble at 4.45pm.*

Incredibly, he scored in the semi-final, though United would go on to lose in the replay. The legend of Cork's facial hair lives on. As a reminder that there was once a time when a man who looked older than your grandad could make it to the pinnacle of the Beautiful Game.

W. G. GRACE
GLOUCESTERSHIRE

The night of April 29th 1996 remains one of the most infamous in Premier League history. After his Newcastle team had scraped a 1-0 win against Leeds, Kevin Keegan faced the cameras to give the most brilliant, bonkers post-match interview of all time.

It was meant to be his Henry V moment, a chance to boost the troops for one final charge unto the breach. In truth, the war was all but over. The Toon were six points behind and the win at Elland Road did little more than prolong the agony. Newcastle's hopes of victory were thinner than Kate Moss's jeans.

Still, with a little encouragement from Sky's erstwhile duo Richard Keys and Andy Gray, it didn't stop King Kevin unleashing one last battle cry:

KK: *"We just want to keep our hopes alive, and a lot of things have been said over the last few days, some of it almost slanderous, and we've never commented. We've just got on working, trying to pass the ball like we do in training."*

RK: *"What do you mean by that? That people have been having a go at you and your team?"*

This is prime Keys. You don't spend years at TV-AM alongside the likes of Anne Diamond, Timmy Mallet and Roland Rat without developing a nose for a story. He smells the controversy brewing here. We're only a few seconds in and he's smashing this.

KK: *"I think you've got to send Alex Ferguson a tape of this game haven't you? Isn't that what he asked for?"*

Interesting that Ferguson should have insisted on a tape being sent to him, as if the live feed direct to his telly wasn't comprehensive enough. We knew he didn't trust Premier League timekeepers, but cameramen too? This is really quite the conspiracy.

AG: *"Well, I'm sure if he was watching tonight, Kevin, he'd have no arguments about the way Leeds went about their job and, really, they tested your team."*

KK: *"And we're playing Notts Forest on Thursday, and he objected to that. Now, that was fixed up four months ago. We were supposed to play Notts Forest. I mean that sort of stuff, we're bigger than that."*

RK: *"That's part and parcel of the psychological battle isn't it, Kevin?"*

More coaxing and cajoling from the hirsute newshound. Wonderful stuff. A sly dig implying Kevin's taking this too seriously. After all, it's just banter isn't it?

KK: *"No, that's... when you do that with footballers, like he said about Leeds, and when you do things like that about a man like Stuart Pearce... I've kept really quiet but I'll tell you something, he went down in my estimation when he said that.*

"We have not resorted to that, but I'll tell you.. you can tell him now if you're watching it: we're still fighting for this title. And he's got to go to Middlesbrough and get something. And... and... I'll tell you, honestly, I will love it if we beat them. Love it."

Unfortunately, like most teams, Manchester United did go to Middlesbrough and get something. A win. And, with that, the Premier League title.

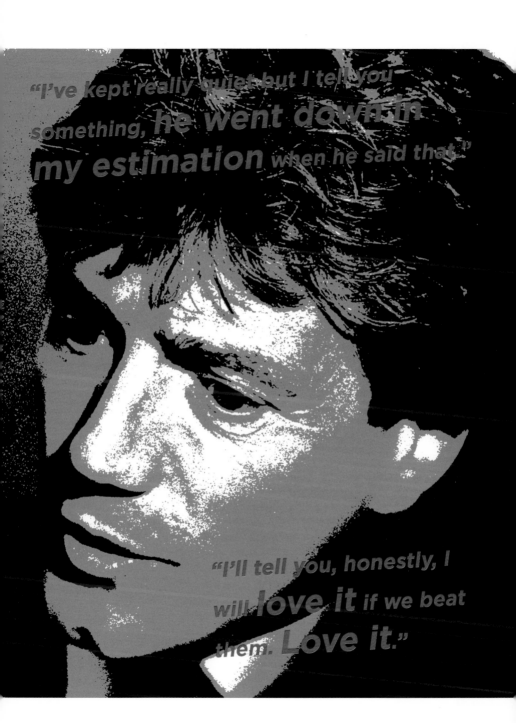

"I've kept really quiet but I tell you something, he went down in my estimation when he said that."

"I'll tell you, honestly, I will love it if we beat them. Love it."

When you're in the gantry, under immense time pressure to narrate what's happening in front of your eyes, you're often told to speak in soundbites. Ron Atkinson went one better; he had his own diction. A dialect entirely of his own creation that celebrated the nuances of association football.

Reducer eg *"That's clever that from Francis Benali. He's put the reducer in on the tricky winger there. Let's see how he responds."*

The most important weapon in a footballer's arsenal. When faced with a more talented or skilful foe, it was important to test them physically, preferably via illegal means. It was the in-game equivalent of a "wet Tuesday night at Stoke". Let's see just how creative they are once they've been two-footed at ankle height.

Little Eyebrows eg *"Merson's whipped it in and Bould's given it the little eyebrows at the front stick."*

In Big Ron's world, the deadliest of set piece routines was a corner whipped in to the near post for a big centre-half to provide the merest flick into the six-yard box where a team-mate would be waiting ready to pounce.

Lollipop eg *"Nice little lollipop from Peter Ndlovu there, to keep the full-back on his toes."*

Big Ron's affectionate term for a stepover. And like the real-life confectionery, it was perfectly acceptable in the right circumstances. But woe betide a winger found guilty of unnecessary or poorly timed lollipops at the expense of getting a cross into the box. Concentrate on your bread and butter, son.

Spotter's Badge eg *"Spotter's badge for Gordon Cowans there with that pass to Dean Saunders."*

The highest form of praise from the big man. This honour was bestowed upon those who showed moments of extraordinary vision during a game of association football. It could be a playmaker threading a through ball, or a midfielder snuffing out danger. Badges weren't handed out willy-nilly. You were lucky to get one or maybe two a game.

Wide-Awake Club eg *"Barry Venison's not in the Wide-Awake Club there. He's switched off and given Big Mick Harford two yards of space."*

Nothing to do with Timmy Mallet, though Ron liked his players to have the endless energy of ITV's popular children's entertainer. Anyone who switched off during a Saturday afternoon (by leaving a striker unmarked, for example) was immediately expected to renew their membership to the Wide-Awake Club on Monday morning.

Hollywood Ball eg *"He's been poor for me, the lad in midfield, Veron. Too many Hollywood passes. He wants to concentrate on keeping the thing."*

Nothing invoked Ron's ire more than a highly ambitious pass that more often than not failed to meet its intended target. It's a simple game, son. Keep it that way.

Of course, it would be remiss to mention that some other choice language, for which he apologised profusely, sadly curtailed Ron's media career. There has been something of a public rehabilitation since and he still retains a place in my heart. Big Ron's voice alongside the magnificent Brian Moore was the perfect accompaniment for many a midweek night on ITV watching the Champions' League: exotic players from exotic places, listening to a man with his own extraordinary take on English prose.

"He's put the **Reducer** *in."*

"Little Eyebrows."

"Nice little **Lollipop.***"*

"Spotter's Badge."

"Not in the **Wide Awake Club** *there."*

"Too many **Hollywood passes."**

In 1998 life was good for Robbie Williams. The cheeky chappie had topped the charts with 'Angels' and cemented his status as a solo artist after his acrimonious transfer from Take That.

In fact, things were going so well that his agent negotiated a cameo appearance on the BBC's World Cup coverage from France. It was a bold move. Pop stars, like footballers, rarely perform well outside of their comfort zones. And should the two ever mix, the results could be disastrous. We've all heard 'Diamond Lights'.

Despite that, the early signs were good. Williams was welcomed on to the sofa by his new gaffer Des Lynam, a man used to managing big characters. When *Match of the Day* unveiled Alan Hansen and Gary Lineker, two men who spent the '80s as arch-rivals on the football pitch, as their new pundit partnership, few thought it would work. Yet Lynam had got the best out of both his new signings. If anyone could integrate a livewire like Williams into the side, it was him.

Unfortunately, he hadn't accounted for his new charge's next move. Whether it was an attempt to secure the spotlight, or a genuine effort to impress his new manager, Williams seized the moment by unveiling a home-made 'DES IS GOD' T-shirt that he'd brought especially for the big occasion. Lynam brushed it off with typical ease. After all, it's hard to argue with the truth.

And it's even harder to argue with Martin O'Neill. The feisty Leicester boss had a reputation for straight talking. His Foxes side was all spit and sawdust. Like his mentor Brian Clough, he didn't suffer big egos, and that no-nonsense approach had made him one of the hottest managerial properties in English football.

So when Williams, with his silly T-shirt and cheeky smile, barged into football's inner sanctum of the punditry studio, O'Neill decided to set him straight:

"To be fair, I think you've done really well because I thought you would struggle after Take That. I really did. You can't play. You can't write. You can't play a guitar. I thought Gary Barlow probably kept the band together. I really thought you would struggle. But the 'Angels' song was top class. Absolutely top class. I have to say that."

Williams managed to smile his way through the experience with the awkwardness of a man undergoing a vasectomy in front of his grandmother. The duo shook hands afterwards but there was no disputing the winner. Williams had been humbled before a live TV audience. That's what happens when you live your life through a lens.

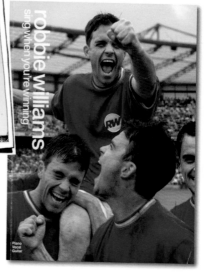

It was October 1994 and Gillingham were struggling. Actually, it was worse than that. Gillingham were crap. Absolute crap. They were near the bottom of the Football League, they had no money, and there were bigger crowds in Our Price than at rickety old Priestfield Stadium.

Staring another relegation battle in the face, you could forgive the chairman for going in search of divine inspiration. Few would imagine that divine inspiration would be a spandex-wearing star of Saturday night television.

Mike van Wijk was the cartoonish villain of ITV's *Gladiators*, where he played the notorious 'Wolf'. Amidst a roster of twentysomething He-Man lookalikes, bursting with suntans and steroids, he was quite the anomaly. At some ten to 15 years older than the rest of the cast, with a receding hairline, thinning ponytail and obligatory freakish muscle, he looked like the offspring of a one-night stand between Status Quo's Francis Rossi and The Incredible Hulk.

However, in the years before he plagued *Gladiators'* notoriously no-nonsense referee John Anderson with his unsportsmanlike behaviour, van Wijk was a decent amateur footballer as well as a Gillingham supporter.

So, when he heard the Gills were down on their luck, he kindly agreed to turn out for the reserves, hopefully put a few hundred extra fans on the gate and boost the Kent club's empty coffers.

> *Amidst a roster of twentysomething He-Men lookalikes he was quite the anomaly.*

The tactic worked a treat. Some 561 hardy souls, which was roughly 560 more than the traditional turnout for a reserve fixture, saw van Wijk (helpfully listed as 'The Wolf' in the matchday programme) play 70 energetic minutes huffing and puffing down the right flank, before hobbling off with injury and then reappearing to sign autographs for his legion of young fans.

It was his one and only outing in a Gills shirt. He wasn't going to swap his dumbbells for Diadoras anytime soon. By anyone's standards, 42 is a tough age to start a football career. And besides, he was already booked to do panto in Woking.

GLADIATORS

ANNUAL 1994

GILLINGHAM			CAMBRIDGE UNITED
Scott Barrett	☐ 1	☐	Chris Roberts
Danny Francis	☐ 2	☐	Andrew Jeffrey
Karl Emerick	☐ 3	☐	Jon Rattle
Andy Ramage	☐ 4	☐	Lenny Pack
Andy Arnott	☐ 5	☐	Junior Hunter
Robin Trott	☐ 6	☐	Marc Joseph
The Wolf	☐ 7	☐	John Fowler
Sean Daly	☐ 8	☐	Danny Granville
Grant Watts	☐ 9	☐	Michael Kyd
Adbul Camara	☐ 10	☐	Leon Gutzmore
John Hooker	☐ 11	☐	Kofi Nyamah
Ian Hutchinson	☐ 12	☐	Mark Barry
Paul Sykes	☐ 14	☐	Russell Stock

Being a professional footballer is a hard enough job. You have to keep yourself at the pinnacle of physical fitness, cope with the burden of expectations, then deliver every Saturday afternoon. In the '90s some club chairmen decided that wasn't quite enough stress to deal with and asked their best players to manage the team, too.

Bryan Robson

Choosing what to wear on your first day of work has long been a source of angst for any new starter. Go too smart and you'll appear too eager to impress. Whereas taking it too casual could make you look like you're only here for the Christmas do and the end-of-year bonus.

In 1993 new Middlesbrough boss Bryan Robson found a unique solution, turning up in both his suit AND matchwear. It was an extraordinary sight. A bit like Clark Kent dashing into a phone box to morph into Superman, only to dash out halfway through because he'd realised he left the oven on.

Luckily 'Captain Marvel' wasn't afflicted by such indecision once he started the job. The new gaffer drove Boro to promotion in his first season in charge and gave the fans some of their most exciting years in the top flight.

Glenn Hoddle

Hoddle's man-management was, by all accounts, rather lacking in compassion. He had the same effect on your confidence as seeing a priest heading for your hospital bed clutching a set of rosary beads.

The problem was that even though Hoddle was no longer physically a top footballer, technically he was still miles better than anyone else. And he knew it. So when he got his first managerial job at second-tier Swindon, it was no surprise

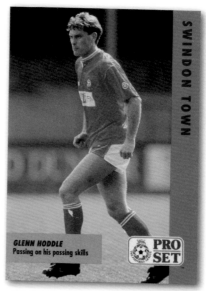

SWINDON TOWN

GLENN HODDLE
Passing on his passing skills

PRO SET

when he named himself in the starting XI. He won promotion via the play-offs with Town, before heading to Chelsea where he would continue to outshine his first team before finally hanging up his boots.

Hoddle, a man of notoriously devout faith, did well at Stamford Brudge but couldn't produce miracles. As the old parable goes, you'll need more than loaves and fishes to turn Paul Furlong into a 20-goal-a-season Premier League striker.

Ruud Gullit

The arrival of Ruud Gullit at Chelsea was the catalyst for the continental invasion of the Premier League. This was a global icon. A man who had revolutionised Serie A with the all-conquering AC Milan side, and powered Holland to the European Championships alongside Frank Rijkaard and Marco Van Basten. Now here he was, in England, patrolling centre midfield with Eddie Newton.

Gullit settled sublimely into his new surroundings. Despite his advancing years, he was comfortably better than everyone else on the pitch. And when Glenn Hoddle got the England job, Gullit was the fans' choice to succeed him. The Dutchman took the Blues to sixth in his first season in charge and won the FA Cup before he was later sacked by Ken Bates, because that's what Ken Bates does.

Attilio Lombardo

Nice man, Steve Coppell. Softly spoken. Not one to brag. It says a lot about Coppell's humility that when he quit his job at Crystal Palace in 1998, having been one of the most successful and popular managers in Selhurst Park history, he thought nothing about suggesting a total novice should replace him.

The outgoing boss recommended Attilio Lombardo for the hot seat. Which seemed like a logical appointment until you considered: (i) he didn't speak the native tongue, and (ii) he didn't want the job.

Anyway, given that Lombardo had the same command of the English language as he did of his hairline, he needed an assistant to translate his philosophy to the team. Step forward Tomas Brolin, the podgy playmaker who had spent the early '90s soaring to the top of the professional

> *Lombardo had the same command of the English language as he did of his hairline.*

game, and the mid '90s eating the rewards.

Lombardo and Brolin trying to resuscitate the corpse of Palace's season sounds like football's version of *Weekend at Bernie's*. And ended with an inevitable tragi-comic result: relegation.

In October of 1992, Sky's much-vaunted Premier League was already in full swing. There was *Super Sunday*, *Monday Night Football*, as well as fireworks and cheerleaders across the land when the cameras rolled into town. The dark days of hooliganism were in the past. This was football's bright new future.

One man who never knowingly shied away from the spotlight was Vinnie Jones. As the proud holder of the worst disciplinary rap sheet in the country, including a world record for receiving a booking (after four seconds), the Wimbledon enforcer sensed the opportunity to jump on the media bandwagon and raise his brand profile in his own unique fashion – by entering the lucrative Christmas video market.

Getting a VHS as a stocking filler was a mandatory for any serious football fan in the '90s. Titles like *101 Great Goals* would be watched on a loop for the entirety of the next 365 days, as impressionable youths would recreate what they saw on screen in parks and playgrounds across the land.

However, no one had ever seen an offering like this. The premise of *Soccer's Hard Men* was Jones celebrating the likes of Ron 'Chopper' Harris, Graeme Souness and Norman Hunter

in 76 minutes of festive football thuggery.

The bigwigs at Soho Square were horrified. They'd spent 20 years trying to clean up football's reputation. Now Vinnie had taken violence off the terraces and put it on to VHS – at Christmas, no less. The thought of familes gathering round the telly after the Queen's speech to watch Vinnie cripple Steve McMahon was simply unpalatable.

The Dons midfielder was given a fine and a suspended sentence for bringing the game into 'disrepute', though the FA were unable to stop the video nasty hitting the shelves. In fact, it became one of the most popular sports videos sold that Christmas.

Maybe it was the controversy behind it that made it such essential viewing. Or maybe it was the charm of watching Vinnie fondly reel off a list of his favourite football infractions, like he's on a shithouse version of *Desert Island Discs*...

Elbowing people in the face, severing their tendons with the soles of your boots and grabbing your opponent by the nutsack. Merry F**king Christmas Everybody. Love from Vinnie Jones.

"You come in with your **studs right down his calf to his achilles.** *That's always a nice one."*

"There's the **poke in the eye** *when your opponent's not looking."*

"Going up for the header, **with the elbow out** *and giving the opponent a nice* **lump behind the ear."**

"You put your opponent down then lift him up, **pull his armpit hairs and he's screaming blue murder."**

"There's the Gazza one where if they get too close to you, **you grab them by the testicles."**

"When the ball's up the other end of the field, **the centre-half lays out the centre-forward with a right-hander."**

In July 1992 John Jensen was living the dream. He'd scored the goal of a lifetime in the European Championships final to give underdogs Denmark (who only joined the tournament as late replacements for war-torn Yugoslavia) a historic victory over the Germans.

Overnight, the midfielder had become a star. A symbol of the most unlikely international result since the Allies held the Nazis to a 4-4 draw with Sylvester Stallone in goal.

Before the tournament, if you'd asked a random football fan to name three things about Denmark, they'd have said Michael Laudrup, bacon... and Michael Laudrup. Now the name John Jensen could be added to that esteemed list.

It helped that he looked memorable, too. With a mop of curly hair and a magnificent moustache, JJ was a triumph of testosterone: the result of a macho lab experiment that successfully fused the DNA of Kevin Keegan with Magnum PI.

He instantly became a hot property in the transfer market. There were rumours of big-money moves to European giants. So when it was announced that Jensen was

DANMARK

JOHN JENSEN

UEFA 92

> **When John Jensen signed for Arsenal, there were ripples of excitement across the English game.**

on his way to Arsenal, there were ripples of excitement across the English game.

This was, of course, the summer of Sky's Whole New Ball Game: the launch of the eagerly-awaited Premier League. At this point there were only a handful of continental names on teamsheets across the top flight (even Eric Cantona was only making occasional appearances from the subs bench at Leeds), so the arrival of a genuine star was seen as quite the coup.

Arsenal fans were understandably giddy with glee. The previous season, David Hillier – who ran around a bit, tackled a bit, and ran around a bit more – had been a mainstay of their midfield. Jensen, the goal-scoring powerhouse of Euro 92, would be a significant improvement. Or so they thought.

Disappointment is the cruellest of human emotions. Mainly because of it's clandestine arrival in your psyche. Tragic events can provoke deep sadness. Just as instantaneous moments can provoke euphoric highs. But disappointment... it creeps up on you. It's like a subconscious erosion of your soul.

In the 97 games after Jensen's arrival, it's hard to pinpoint exactly when Arsenal fans felt truly disappointed. Any new signing is given a period of grace. And more so when that signing arrives from foreign pastures. There was a catalogue of excuses: "just needs time to settle in" and "just needs to find his feet".

But as the days, weeks and months went by, the concerns about Jensen grew louder and bolder. Soon, it was less a question of him finding his feet, as to whether his feet were worth finding in the first place. No one questioned Jensen's commitment. The Dane showed plenty of that. From the first whistle he ran around a bit, tackled a bit, then ran around a bit more. All of which sounded strangely familiar.

And then there was the shooting. The terrible, terrible shooting. The sight of Jensen teeing up a strike at goal soon provoked panic in the North Bank.

By New Year's Eve 1994, that sense of fear had long gone as ball after ball disappeared into the north London skyline, usually met with a chorus of groans and laughter.

> ❝❝ *The sight of him teeing up a strike at goal soon provoked panic in the North Bank.* ❞❞

Besides, there weren't many people to aim at any more. In the League, Arsenal were rotten. George Graham was on his way out and fans weren't making their way in. There were only 32,393 hardy souls in attendance for the final fixture of the calendar year at home to QPR.

Outside, amongst the usual gaggle of street vendors, even the trade for the ever-hopeful 'I Was There When Jensen Scored' T-shirts was starting to dwindle. By now, the cruel weight of disappointment had crushed every Arsenal fan's sense of optimism. It was never going to happen.

Until it finally did.

In the 64th minute, with Arsenal trailing to a Bradley Allen goal, Jensen picked up the ball on the left flank, comprehensively beat his man and curled a delicious strike into the top far corner of the net. Cue delirium. Highbury erupted as the pent-up frustration of seeing every second of Jensen's goal famine was finally released.

That's the thing about disappointment. As long as it takes to appear, it can be banished in seconds. The misery of those 97 mediocre games was forgotten. This was John Jensen. The Danish enforcer. The midfield general. He'd finally found his feet. And now, watch him go. He was going to drive Arsenal on to glory. Nothing could stop him.

The Gunners lost 3-1. Jensen played another 41 games for Arsenal. Ran around a lot, tackled a lot, and ran around a lot more. But never scored again.

At least the T-shirt sellers did well out of it. The shirts became a collector's item at Highbury. As they did at Loftus Road, where the return fixture saw Arsenal's travelling faithful greeted with hordes of Rangers' fans wearing tees saying: 'I Was There When Jensen Scored... And Allen, Gallen and Impey'.

The '90s were a golden age for English strikers. Behind every Premier League goalkeeper there was typically a ball freshly delivered from Alan Shearer, Ian Wright, Les Ferdinand, Andy Cole or Teddy Sheringham. Meanwhile, in the red half of Merseyside, they had their own folk hero. Robbie Fowler, a young talent from Toxteth, had filled the sizeable goalscoring boots of the legendary Ian Rush.

His fabled finishing ability had earned the nickname 'God' from the Kop. And whatever your religious sensitivities, it seemed a fair bet that if you did throw Fowler a bunch of loaves and fishes, they'd still end up in the top corner.

The one accolade that eluded the star striker was a victory over Everton. Toffees fans taunted their star rival at every turn, including unfounded allegations about recreational drug use, which angered him immensely. So when Fowler scored twice in the 1999 Merseyside derby he celebrated by dropping to his knees and snorting the white line triumphantly in front of the Everton fans. The Reds won the game 3-2 but afterwards all the talk was about Liverpool's number nine.

You could hear the bums squeaking at English football's HQ. The game's administrator had endured a rocky few years. The heady days of Sir Bert Millichip and Graham Kelly sitting in their oak office, presiding over the FA Cup draw with all the enthusiasm of men debating the merits of a new cordless drill, were long gone. Sir Bert had retired to the golf course, whilst Kelly and fellow FA bigwig Keith Wiseman had resigned in disgrace over a 'loan' to the Football Association of Wales (FAW), allegedly in return for their support to get Kelly and co. a seat on FIFA's prized executive board.

Now was a chance for the English game's

Fowler crosses the line
England striker in trouble again after 'snorting' gesture inflames Merseyside derby – Page 3

custodians to spring into action. We couldn't have one of the Premier League's brightest stars besmirching the reputation of the Beautiful Game. Justice would need to be dispensed. Quickly.

In fairness, it was an open and shut case. Even the FA couldn't cock this up. This was Fowler giving his terrace tormentors the middle finger. And he'd have to take a slap on the wrist for it. *Brought the game into disrepute. Sorry. Accept the fine. Move on.*

But Liverpool's Gerard Houllier had other idea, coming up with an excuse so implausible even OJ Simpson would have thought twice about using it.

"He was eating the grass. It is a Cameroonian gesture that Rigobert Song has taught him after he scores in training," insisted the Anfield boss with all the confidence of a snail crossing the M1.

Predictably, the FA laughed this off this pathetic line of defence, issuing Fowler with a four-game ban and a hefty £32,000 fine. After all, what did Houllier take them for? Imbeciles?

As if Rigobert Song's ever scored a f**king goal in training...

In the days before false nines, there was no better attacking plan than getting the ball wide and slinging it into the mixer. If you did, these were the type of men you wanted on the end of it.

Duncan Ferguson

We got our first glimpse of Big Dunc's aerial prowess during his early years at Rangers, when a headbutt on Raith's John McStay earned him a prison sentence. It was his fourth conviction after a bizarre

was football's answer to a battering ram. At 6'4", there were players who matched him for height, though no other could rival his unquenchable thirst for violence. His tally of eight red cards meant he was a frequent visitor to the FA.

He mellowed somewhat in his later years (though a nice little chokehold on Steffen Freund meant he kept his toe in the disciplinary waters) and let his ability do the talking. His hat-trick of headers (v Bolton in 1997) made him a permanent

FA CUP SIXTH ROUND (Sponsored by Littlewoods Pools)
EVERTON v NEWCASTLE UNITED
Sunday 12th March 1995   Kick-Off 3.00pm   Price £1.50

> *After his 44-day sojourn at Her Majesty's Pleasure, Ferguson moved to Everton and became an icon.*

pub quiz question. His 68 goals, and the countless battered egos of opposition centre-halves he left in his wake, made him a Premier League legend.

DUNCAN FERGUSON

spate of off-pitch affray during his late teens that saw him cautioned for (separate) attacks on a policeman, a fisherman and a postman (who was on crutches, just for good measure). After his 44-day sojourn at Her Majesty's Pleasure, Ferguson moved to Everton and became an icon.

There were few more exhilarating sights in the '90s than a ball being whipped into the box at Goodison Park and Duncan Ferguson charging towards it. The Scot

And, in a remarkable twist of fate, Ferguson would later redeem the criminal record of his wayward youth. In 2001 two burglars, quite possibly the most ill-informed of their profession, invaded his

family home in Lancashire – and instantly regretted it. Dunc battered them both, and one of the intruders spent three days in hospital before he was convicted.

Maybe those centre-halves got off lightly, after all.

Kevin Francis

There was a spell during the mid '90s where journalists were legally obliged to prefix the name 'Kevin Francis' with '6'7" striker'. In extreme circumstances, or where variation was editorially required, there were other acceptable descriptions: 'Big striker Kevin Francis' or 'Beanpole striker Kevin Francis' were always good

options. 'Towering striker Kevin Francis' was useful for more dramatic moments, but the rule was clear for all to see: indicator of height + position = Stockport's Kevin Francis.

> *Even the affable Ray Wilkins said, "If I need any guttering done, I'll give him a call."*

It was a simple but effective formula, which was rather like the man himself. 'Big Kev', as he was affectionately known by the local press accustomed to his huge frame, became a goalscoring sensation at Edgeley Park. Hatters boss Danny Bergara is credited with 'spotting' Francis in a game for Derby reserves, which is a bit like patting yourself on the back for noticing Bigfoot having a shit in your back garden.

Francis scored a mightily impressive 117 goals in four seasons at Stockport, propelling them into the second tier. Despite his exploits, his status as the tallest player in England made him a figure of fun amongst opposition fans, at least until he inevitably scored against them. Indeed, after Big Kev knocked QPR out of the FA Cup, even eternally affable Rangers boss Ray Wilkins couldn't help himself. "If I need any guttering done, I'll give him a call," he said.

The Big Fella's remarkable form earned him a move to Birmingham where Barry Fry's 'Get it, hoof it, head it' tactics suited his talents perfectly. Promotion to the First Division was secured, and Francis terrorised top-tier opponents Middlesbrough and Leeds in a memorable run to the 1996 League Cup semi-finals.

These days, he's a policeman in Canada. Criminals in Calgary – be warned: You can't escape the long legs of the law.

Carl Leaburn

Mention the name Carl Leaburn in certain parts of South London and there's a fair chance you'll get something of a misty-eyed response. Charlton and Wimbledon fans alike have fond memories of the imposing striker, though very few can recall him actually scoring.

Much like a stubborn koi carp, Leaburn had something of a distant relationship with the net. During eleven years at Charlton he averaged less than five goals

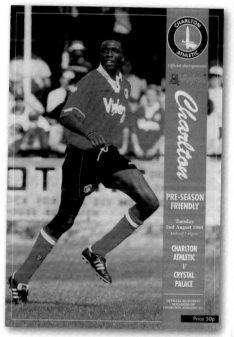

Leaburn's extraordinary work-rate. Big strikers were routinely criticised for their lack of energy and mobility, traits Leaburn had in abundance.

He was a manager's dream: running for everything and contesting every ball. And his size (a healthy 6'3" and 13st) made him a general nuisance in the penalty area, despite the fact that he offered so very little genuine goal threat.

I suppose it's like someone rolling a defused World War II bomb into your

> **Charlton and Dons fans have fond memories of the imposing striker, though few can recall him actually scoring.**

front room. You know deep down that it's not going to harm you, but there's no f**king way you're going to take your eyes off it.

Anyway, Leaburn's many strike partners over the years benefitted from his selflessness and he was credited with countless assists, which suited his humble nature. Even when Charlton fans proudly wore 'I Saw Leaburn Score' T-shirts at The Valley, it was meant with genuine affection rather than scorn.

per campaign. And three seasons at the Dons yielded a spectacular tally of four successful efforts on goal. That's 1.33 recurring per year. On numbers alone, it's hard to think of a man so incredibly bad at his job who remained so popular. In that respect, he was football's version of Inspector Gadget.

Yet that does a great disservice to

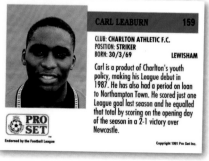

CARL LEABURN 159

CLUB: CHARLTON ATHLETIC F.C.
POSITION: STRIKER
BORN: 30/3/69 LEWISHAM

Carl is a product of Charlton's youth policy, making his League debut in 1987. He has also had a period on loan to Northampton Town. He scored just one League goal last season and he equalled that total by scoring on the opening day of the season in a 2-1 victory over Newcastle.

PRO SET
Endorsed by the Football League
Copyright 1991 Pro Set Inc.

Being a teenager in the '90s was sensational. Buying alcopops with fake IDs, drinking in the playground at the park, listening to indie music. And best of all, you could do all of that whilst unashamedly wearing white jeans. What a time to be alive.

If you were a teenage boy during that era there's a fair chance that whilst you were making your way through your third Bacardi Breezer, your mind occasionally wandered to what the future may hold. Perhaps a dream of scoring in front of a packed Premier League crowd. Or owning the stage at Knebworth. The depressing reality was probably a variety of crappy temp roles and a deeply underwhelming office job.

But a lad could dream. Or, in Paul McGregor's case, he could live the dream.

In 1995, the rookie striker was thrust into the headlines after scoring the winner for Nottingham Forest v Lyon in the UEFA Cup, live on the BBC. He was an instant media sensation. Not merely for his age, but for his appearance. McGregor didn't look like your typical footballer. With long blonde hair, sideburns and an unmistakable swagger, he looked more like a f**king rock 'n' roll star.

Because he was.

You see, whilst most footballers were spending their afternoons in the pub or snooker hall, McGregor would be jamming with his Britpop band, Merc, and headlining at Nottingham's own Rock City on a gig promoted by the notorious lads' mag, *Loaded*.

McGregor himself soon became a feature in magazines and popular culture, whether it was in *90 Minutes*, or sitting on the sofa on *Soccer AM*. He was unlike anything we'd ever seen before. Football and music had always had a tragi-comic relationship. By the mid '90s we were still recovering from the monstrosity of Gazza and Lindisfarne doing 'Fog on the Tyne'. Frankly, we were used to hearing stories of footballers smashing up taxi drivers, not watching Smashing Pumpkins.

Remarkably, McGregor was actually good. At both. He was equally comfortable scoring wonder goals at Old Trafford and then owning the stage at a packed gig.

There were rumours that his manager Frank Clark, who'd given him his first-team opportunity and a bumper new contract, was worried that music was a distraction. Mind you, Clark was a worrier by trade. He wore the permanent expression of a man who'd just found a melted choc ice in his back pocket.

> **Whilst most footballers spent their afternoons in the pub or snooker hall, McGregor would be jamming with his Britpop band, Merc.**

On this occasion, perhaps he was right. For, as quickly as McGregor rose to fame, he then disappeared. A nasty knee injury and change of manager meant he lost his way at Forest. And despite winning Player of the Year at his next club, Plymouth Argyle, his career started to slide away after that. At least on the pitch. However, unlike other retired pros, he didn't swap Parklife for Porklife. Instead, McGregor turned his attention full time to music, and achieved further success. His new band, Ulterior, played gigs across the world to some acclaim.

To the '90s football connoisseur, he remains one of the most recognisable faces of the decade – when indie music and football were part of the British zeitgeist.

And though he may have only played a handful of games, the former Forest striker's legacy remains. He was the first – and only – Britpop footballer. If you'd asked any teenager in 1995 whether they'd swap places with McGregor, they'd definitely, maybe say 'yes'.

What's the right way to play football? It's a question that no one has ever really answered. We often hear pundits pat losing teams on the back with a "well, at least they play the right way," as if that should soften the blow of defeat. That's all well and good, son. But pats on the back don't pay the bills. Results do. John Beck taught us that.

In the early '90s, Beck took over as manager of Cambridge United and immediately instilled his own, unique, footballing ethos. There was indeed a 'right way' to play the Beautiful Game: beat the eleven bastards standing in front of you.

He championed the 'simplicity is genius' mantra, a slogan which he pasted all around the Cambridge training ground, including on the back of the toilet doors.

Quite how you can over-complicate sitting on the khazi is debatable, though Beck was nothing if not meticulous.

From his first day in the job, he gave the U's, then floundering in the basement division with a poor team and poor crowds, a much-needed sense of direction and identity: they were going to get promoted. And they were going to do it by being total shithouses.

The new gaffer wasn't here to win friends. He was here to win football matches. And as a keen student of statistics and probabilities, he'd worked out his own formula to guarantee three points on a Saturday afternoon.

Despite his many detractors – Beck was nicknamed 'Dracula' for supposedly sucking the life out of football – his robotic

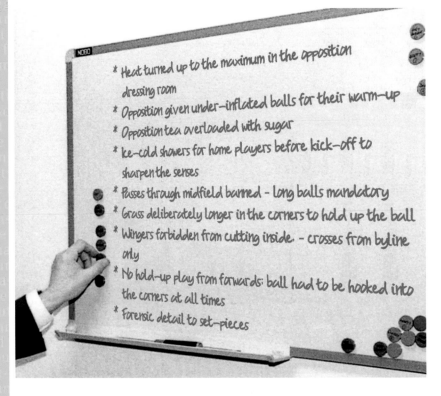

* Heat turned up to the maximum in the opposition dressing room
* Opposition given under-inflated balls for their warm-up
* Opposition tea overloaded with sugar
* Ice-cold showers for home players before kick-off to sharpen the senses
* Passes through midfield banned – long balls mandatory
* Grass deliberately longer in the corners to hold up the ball
* Wingers forbidden from cutting inside. – crosses from byline only
* No hold-up play from forwards; ball had to be hooked into the corners at all times
* Forensic detail to set-pieces

approach worked wonders. Cambridge rose rapidly through the leagues, spearheaded by the statuesque strikeforce of Dion Dublin and John Taylor. Indeed, at one stage they were within 90 minutes of the Premier League, where their presence would have ruffled more feathers than Godzilla in a henhouse.

As is often the case, dictatorial regimes like this last only so long before the gentry start to revolt. Steve Claridge was substituted early in a particular game for having the temerity to complete a one-two with one of his team-mates. And others suffered similar infractions for daring to a pass to feet.

Such idiosyncracies were tolerated by the squad whilst they were winning games. But when they hit a sticky patch in the second tier, as teams had the chance to develop more sophisticated responses to Beck's aerial Blitzkrieg, the players came to lose faith. Despite their protestations, Beck refused to budge on his principles and eventually lost his job, never to repeat his success elsewhere.

These days, Cambridge have tumbled out of the League and back again, whilst Beck has experienced something of an unlikely

JOHN BECK
Successfully gained successive promotions

PRO SET

recovery. Despite his subsequent failures at managerial level, he eventually landed a job with the Football Association, where he educates the next generation of football coaches. We've not seen the training materials, but maybe deep within the modules on high pressing, zonal marking and passing through lines, an element of Beck-ism still remains...

... If all else fails, just get the ball in the f**king mixer.

As football became increasingly fashionable in the 1990s, it was inevitable that many a public figure looking to boost their profile would find tenuous ways to associate themselves with the Beautiful Game.

There were the genuine examples, of course. No one doubted Danny Baker's passion for Millwall, or Nigel Kennedy's affiliation with Aston Villa.

But there were a few eyebrows raised when Tony Blair professed his convenient love for Newcastle United, given that Kevin Keegan's side were very much the flavour of the month in the middle of the decade. In fairness, Blair stuck to his allegiance even when the Toon deteriorated into an administrative mess that wasted millions on over-hyped rubbish like Stephane Guivarc'h. Which may explain his fondness for the Millennium Dome.

> **There were utterly bizarre football affiliations that defied explanation.**

And then there were the utterly bizarre football affiliations that defied explanation. Unions so unusual or unforeseen, and often unearthed on live telly, that we can only bask in their batshit craziness.

Shawn Michaels (The Blackburn Rovers)
In spring of 1995 the title race was hotting up. On a Super Sunday in April, Kenny Dalgish's Rovers travelled to Upton Park to face a West Ham side battling relegation. Amongst the Lancashire faithful, at least in spirit, was a man who had travelled further than most to see his team play. WWF superstar Shawn Michaels, aka 'The Heartbreak Kid', appeared pitchside for

SHAWN MICHAELS*

an interview with intrepid Sky reporter Nick Collins to discuss his love of 'The Blackburn Rovers'.

In his distinct Texan drawl, the wrestler described how a 'distant relative' had links to Blackburn, therefore sparking his new-found allegiance. Which sounds similar to the level of scrutiny applied to Andy Townsend's international career.

Ever the pro, Collins wisely kept the chat nice and light, perhaps for fear of exposing the grappling star's lack of knowledge. Michaels generally spent his weekends battling the likes of Bret 'Hitman' Hart and Yokozuna, so it was difficult to imagine him finding the time to examine the finer points of Stuart Ripley's wing play.

Michaels joined a list of celebrity Rovers fans that included snooker champ Stephen Hendry, *Bullseye* legend Jim Bowen, motor racing's Carl Fogarty and politician Jack Straw. If nothing else, that would have made one hell of a five-a-side team.

After Michaels witnessed his team

lose 2-0, he returned Stateside to resume his day job of kicking, elbowing and clotheslining his opponents into submission. Perhaps he should have spoken to Stuart Ripley after all. That poor bastard had just spent 90 painful minutes up against Julian Dicks.

Naseem Hamed (Sheffield Wednesday AND Sheffield United)

In the mid '90s, there was no hotter Sky property than 'Prince' Naseem Hamed. The Sheffield boxer was everything Murdoch's empire wanted in a star: he was egocentric, controversial and publicity-hungry. But that's quite enough about Richard Keys.

History tells us there's a fine line between being 'charismatic' and being 'a bit of a twat'. And it was a line that Hamed walked daily. Nonetheless, Sky made no apologies for putting the disco-dancing, somersaulting Prince front and centre of their promotional hype.

Hamed's manager Frank Warren, looking to seize on his client's commercial profile, decided to place him on the sofa of BBC's *Fantasy Football League* for possibly the most awkward boxing-football encounter since Henry Cooper's unintentional homo-eroticism with Kevin Keegan, courtesy of their close friends at Brut.

> ## Hamed defied all convention by blithely supporting two arch-rivals.

Hamed quickly grew weary of hosts Skinner and Baddiel, who had queried his football allegiance. "Sheffield," was Hamed's answer. "United and Wednesday. And when they play each other, I'm neutral. I support Sheffield, me."

Once again, here was Hamed defying all known convention, this time by blithely supporting two arch-rivals. It's a good job Warren hadn't booked him on the *Timewatch* episode about World War II. "I'm a big fan of the Allies. But I've got a soft spot for the Reich. I just support humans, me."

Lennox Lewis (West Ham, Crystal Palace and... everyone, basically)

In the early days of *Monday Night Football*, no expense was spared to present this new weekly soccer showpiece. There were cheerleaders, fireworks and – on a balmy day in August 1992 – a guest appearance by heavyweight boxer Lennox Lewis.

The reigning British, European and Commonwealth champion was at Carrow Road to watch the high-flying Canaries face Nottingham Forest. During the interview Lewis was pressed on where his allegiances lay, and duly professed his admiration for a host of sides. "I like West Ham, Arsenal and Crystal Palace, all the London teams," he said.

We perhaps shouldn't have been surprised by the Champ's mixed loyalties. He was, after all, a man who represented Canada in the Olympic Games and was now reinventing himself as Britain's next heavyweight hope, thereby supplanting the inimitable Frank Bruno.

If you're going to try and take on Our Frank in the national popularity stakes, you need as many friends as possible. So liking absolutely EVERYTHING is probably a wise strategy. Maybe that's why he never got to make an appearance on *Desert Island Discs*. "Eight songs? Eight! How about 800?"

> **If you're going to try and take on Our Frank in the popularity stakes, you need as many friends as possible.**

Anyway, Lewis's indecision seemed to spread to his fashion. Sporting a flat-top and a multi-coloured monstrosity of a jacket, he looked like he was auditioning for a part in *The Fresh Prince of Bel-Air*. In the studio, Richard Keys, unusually underdressed in a black suit for a man of such garish tastes, seized the opportunity

to take the high ground: "Heavyweight Champion Lennox Lewis there. I'm not going to tell him that's a silly cardigan," he said. Quite.

During a decade of dominance, Lewis went on to accrue as many belts as he did football clubs. And on a raucous Las Vegas night in November 1999, roared on by an army of travelling Brits, he became the Undisputed Heavyweight Champion of the World by beating Evander Holyfield.

Weeks later he was involved in another prestigious title tilt, this time at the BBC Sports Personality of the Year Awards. It felt like an acid test for his achievements. Henry Cooper had been the last pugilist to pick up the prized gong, way back in 1970. And up against the likes of David Beckham and Colin Jackson, Lewis would need more than the phone calls of London's collective football fanbase to seal a victory.

In the event, he earned another unanimous decision. Finally, he'd won the nation's hearts.

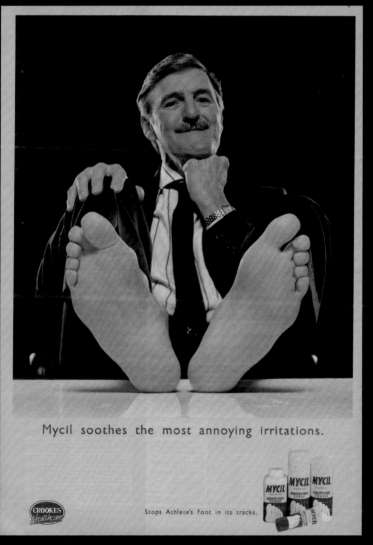

Mycil soothes the most annoying irritations.

Stops Athlete's Foot in its tracks.

Dear old Jimmy. A man never afraid of speaking his mind. Though some might say it was a nice change to see him without his foot in his mouth.

STRIKE PARTNERSHIPS

In the '90s, if you'd asked me what a 'false nine' was, I'd probably have pointed to Stephane Guivarc'h's abominable spell at Newcastle United, when he looked like he'd had his feet surgically replaced with feather dusters.

These days, it's very much a term that's *de rigueur*. And like 'inverted wingers', it has sadly contributed to the demise of one of the vanguards of association football: the front two. For years, it was sacrosanct that a team was only as successful as their front men. Those front men typically adhered to very specific rules: one had to link the play, the other (preferably smaller) man would run in behind.

The '90s was the last decade of the strike partnership. And there were some corkers.

Shearer & Sutton

In his early years at Blackburn, Alan Shearer had enjoyed a fruitful partnership with veteran Mike Newell. The elder man did all the graft, allowing Shearer to grab all the glory. It was enough to get Blackburn into Europe, but ambitious owner Jack Walker wanted more: the Premier League title.

Newell was like the cosy armchair that had never let you down. Until age took its toll. And when Newell started running at the same speed as that cosy armchair, it was time for an upgrade. Enter Chris Sutton for £5 million from Norwich, to the begrudging acceptance of Alan Shearer.

It's a bit like Batman and Superman. Bruce Wayne obviously had a soft spot for Robin, the alleged Boy Wonder. And the Dynamic Duo sold a lot of comics. But if you want to save the universe, it's better to have that big bastard with the cape on your side rather than against you.

As a partnership, they went against all conventional wisdom. Playing two strapping target men up front was unheard

of. Yet it worked perfectly for Blackburn's 'get the ball wide and get it in the mixer' philosophy. Wingers Jason Wilcox and Stuart Ripley supplied more crosses than a Transylvanian timber yard.

Whilst the 'SAS' aces weren't best mates, they were a fearsome force in the Premier League. A combination of 49 League goals (34 for Shearer, 15 for Sutton) propelled Rovers to a famous title win.

Beardsley & Cole

When Peter Beardsley returned to Newcastle as part of the Kevin Keegan revolution, there were a few eyebrows raised at the wisdom of paying £1.5 million for a man in his mid 30s.

Keegan insisted it was excellent value, as Beardsley remained one of the most intelligent footballers in the League. You wouldn't think it to look at him – he looked like the sort of man who thought an innuendo was an Italian suppository. On the pitch, however, the former England striker was as sharp as ever.

Beardsley was paired up front with the raw energy of Andrew Cole, a former Arsenal youth player who had been shipped off to Bristol City and bagged goals galore in the second tier before joining the Magpies.

Age and youth aren't always perfect bedfellows. Just ask Anne Boleyn. On this occasion, however, the two worked in perfect harmony. Between them they netted 65 goals in all competitions, and the Toon finished third in their inaugural Premier League season, qualifying for the UEFA Cup in the process.

Wright & Bright

The Crystal Palace resurgence of the late '80s/early '90s was fuelled by two unlikely star strikers. Mark Bright had a dreadful spell at Leicester where he looked about as comfortable as a penguin on a sunbed. Meanwhile, Wright had been turning out for non-league Greenwich Borough for the princely sum of 30 quid a week.

United by Steve Coppell, the duo hit it off immediately despite being opposites as

players and people. The mild-mannered Bright was a traditional target man. Meanwhile, the explosive Wright – whose legendary temper made the Incredible Hulk look like Mary Poppins – was an inventive and instinctive finisher, who scored goals of considerable quality in ample quantity.

On the pitch their partnership brought promotion to the top flight and an FA Cup final appearance, and both players topped 100 goals for the club before departing for pastures new.

For all the talk these days of money and greed, one thing that hasn't changed is football's primary currency: hope. It's the hope that drags you back in, even when your heart can take no more. It's the hope that means at 2.59pm on the first day of the season, for a fleeting moment, we all believe that anything is possible. Dreams can become reality. Minnows can become giants. Then the whistle blows and the hope extinguishes into a puff of disappointment.

What price do we put on hope?

Back in the '90s, ClubCall gave us the answer. All you needed was a landline and the billpayer's permission, then for the tidy sum of 48 English pence per minute you could get the hottest of hot gossip from your club.

This included exclusive updates from managers, in-depth interviews with top, top players, and live match commentaries from inside the ground. This was football's PS (Pre-Stelling) era, when the only televised sport you got on a Saturday afternoon was rugby league on *Grandstand*, and a host of weary men would routinely crowd round the windows of Dixon's in the high street at 4.45pm to get a glimpse of the final scores.

If you were lucky enough to be sat in the comfort of your own home, then your

only other outlet for live commentary was Radio 5, which was fine if you were a fan of one of the top-flight clubs. But if you were desperate for news from Walsall's trip to Gillingham, then you were out of luck.

There was Teletext, of course. Though updates were very much dependent on the spec of your television. On the big telly

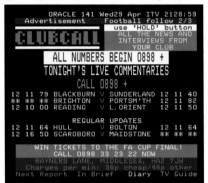

in our house, the pages turned with all the finesse of Freddy Krueger thumbing through *Reader's Digest*. Suddenly, that 48p per minute seemed quite reasonable.

All you wanted was to get into the cut and thrust of the action. You were ready to pay through the nose for it, and ClubCall knew it. There were certainly tight controls on overheads. Sometimes that commentary from the Bescot Stadium sounded like it was coming from a dormant World War II bunker. At other times, the audio was so garbled you wondered if someone had switched the feed with an audio recreation of the Blitz.

Generally, the voices were passionate and unashamedly biased. Part of the thrill of tuning in was hearing an unpolished accent similar to your own painting a vivid picture of the action. The only thing missing was the scoreline. It was the inherent skill of a ClubCall commentator to go ten minutes of play without ever revealing the score in the match. Before you knew it, you'd spaffed a fiver getting excited about the prospect of a consolation goal in a 4-1 drubbing at the hands of Huddersfield Town.

Aside from cutting-edge matchday coverage, where ClubCall really came into its own was transfer news. Because, after all, nothing gives a football fan hope like a new signing. And the marketing men at ClubCall knew just how to exploit it.

Now, in a civilised society, none of us wilfully wish harm on our fellow man. However, there is a special place in Hell for ClubCall headline writers. Not since the Pet Shop Boys stormed the charts with their synthesizers have men with keyboards wielded so much power over the nation's happiness. Reading "SHOCK TRANSFER SWOOP" or "STAR STRIKER ON HIS WAY?" was like injecting adrenaline directly into your aorta. Resistance was futile. No reasonable football fan could ever stop themselves from dialling in. Yes, you knew it was probably bollocks. After all, Clive Wilson was a good full-back, but was he good enough that Gheorghe Hagi was ready to jet in to Loftus Road to solve QPR's left-sided problem? Surely not.

> ## No reasonable football fan could ever stop themselves from dialling in.

Yet what if it was true? It must be worth sparing a few bob to find out? These shameless, irresistible tactics parted fans with millions of pounds of income. At its height, ClubCall was receiving thousands upon thousands of calls per day. It was only when Tim Berners-Lee got his arse in

gear and created the internet that things started to change.

Suddenly, football news and transfer tittle-tattle was at your fingertips. And most importantly, it was free. So you could just plug your dial-up connection to your

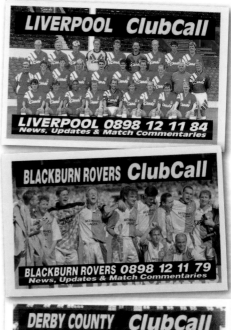

phone socket, click on that news story with all the pop-ups for William Hill, and read to your heart's content about Roberto Baggio, currently being touted as the unlikely replacement for John McGinlay at Bolton Wanderers.

Who's the mug now?

Italia 90 brought us many unlikely unions: Pavarotti and football, Roger Milla and the corner flag, Frank Rijkaard's saliva and Rudi Voller's hair. At the top of the list was Jack Charlton and The Pope: the man overseeing the collective faith of humanity coming face to face with the man who had somehow transformed Ireland into a competitive force on the international scene.

In many ways they were charged with performing miracles in their own right. Albeit with slightly different resources. The leader of the Catholic Church had the wisdom of the Old and New Testaments; Big Jack relied more on the *Rothman's Football Yearbook.*

The Gaffer's recruitment policy at Lansdowne Road consisted of ringing every professional footballer in the top divisions and asking if he fancied a pint of Guinness. It had unearthed some unlikely treasures. Crafty cockney Andy Townsend, who sounded about as Irish as Barbara Windsor, gleefully discovered his distant Gaelic heritage. So too did Tony Cascarino, the striker with the London accent and an Italian surname, who qualified courtesy of his grandpa's birthplace. It later transpired that it wasn't his real grandfather, and Cascarino had closer biological links to Franco Baresi than he did Frank Stapleton, but let's not sweat the small stuff.

In any case, Charlton's ragtag bunch continued to upset football's accepted world order at Italia 90 by holding their own with both England and Holland in the group stages. Ahead of their second-round fixture, Big Jack gave his lads an extra incentive: a win over Romania would

be rewarded with a meeting with the Pope himself. So when David O'Leary knocked in the winning penalty in the shoot-out, it was time for a meeting with his Holiness.

When you think of Jack Charlton's natural habitat, there are certain scenarios that instantly come to mind: relaxing with a cigarette (still in full kit) after a hard Saturday afternoon, sitting on the banks of the River Tyne indulging his endless passion for fishing, or yelling furiously at Steve Staunton to get it in the mixer to Big Niall Quinn.

Sitting in a three-and-a-half hour sermon whilst the supreme pontiff ruminates on the Bible's teachings isn't one of them. That's not to say that Jack wasn't one for a spot of quiet contemplation on the meaning of life. But if he was going to do it, he'd be sat in a deckchair with a decent f**king chance of catching trout for his dinner.

It was no surprise when the Gaffer started to nod off, though erstwhile assistant Maurice Setters was there to nudge him back into consciousness when the drudgery became too much to bear. In fairness, he'd done much the same during the Republic's game with England three weeks earlier.

What did come as something of a revelation was The Pope's affinity with stalwart keeper Packie Bonner. It transpired that Pope John Paul II had been a semi-professional goalie in his native Poland, and as such promised "to keep a special eye out for you", when he chatted to Bonner ahead of the quarter-final with hosts Italy.

If only Bonner had kept a special eye out for the ball, then Ireland might have made it further in the competition. His mistake – spilling a routine shot into the path of Toto Schillaci – cost them the game.

Afterwards, Big Jack did the decent thing

PACKIE SAVES WITH IRISH PERMANENT

IRISH PERMANENT
The People's Choice

and refused to apportion any blame to his loyal custodian.

"Thank you for all you've done," he said to the deflated dressing room after the match. "You couldn't have given me any more. I'm proud of each and every one of you. The country are so proud of what you've done too. Go on, Packie, get yourself in the shower."

It was a masterclass in man-management. Another example of why his team loved him. After a disconsolate Bonner made his way to the bathroom, Jack sat himself down and took a long drag on his cigarette. These instances, trapped in the heartbreak of defeat, are when footballers need an injection of faith more than most. And Big Jack knew that.

Sensing the moment, he took one last reflective puff of his fag, turned to Andy Townsend and said: "Andy, the f**king Pope would have saved that."

Now that's what you call divine inspiration.

"**M**y missus fancies him. Even I don't know whether to play him or f**k him," said Harry Redknapp in reference to the latest addition to his multinational West Ham squad.

He was welcoming Daniel Da Cruz Carvalho, the Portuguese forward who had been the undisputed star of the 1995 FIFA World Youth Championship, and then caught the eye in a senior friendly between Portugal and England a few months later.

Now, one of the most talked-about talents in football was on his way to the Premier League. And it wasn't just his gifted left peg that had made Sandra Redknapp's heart flutter.

You see, Dani was a dreamboat. Hair like Johnny Depp and puppy-dog eyes that could melt the heart of both man and beast. At 19 years of age, he was living every teenager's fantasy. He was both a male model and a top-class international footballer. His arrival at Upton Park – on loan from Sporting Lisbon – sexed up a forward line that had previously been a mixture of the good, the bad and the downright ugly.

Tony Cottee was the team's only reliable source of goals. A Dutchman called Marco Boogers, signed on the basis of VHS footage, had been a total disaster. Realising his mistake, Redknapp brought back the familiar, if somewhat unforgettable face of Iain Dowie. His return to east London, after a brief spell in 1991, was greeted with the same sort of enthusiasm as the police knocking on Violet Kray's front door.

The Irishman lived down to expectations. No one faulted his effort. He huffed, he puffed, and could happily chase a ball for hours on end. Mind you, so could my nan's dog – but you wouldn't rely on an ageing cocker spaniel for Premier League safety.

By February, Dowie had scored just five goals, and with his side hovering just above the relegation zone, Harry Redknapp persuaded the chairman it was time to dip into the transfer market. In came Dreamboat Dani.

The Odd Couple

The Portuguese was thrown straight into the starting eleven for a derby at Spurs, forming a new-look forward line with Dowie. You had to feel for the young lad. Here he was, the sexiest footballer on God's Earth, making his debut alongside a man who looked like he'd spent his youth chasing parked cars.

If Dani was having second thoughts about his career choices, he showed no signs of it. He scored the winner and was named Man of the Match, receiving a bottle of bubbly from strike partner Dowie in a memorable post-match interview on Sky Sports where the broadcaster

Hair like Johnny Depp and puppy-dog eyes that could melt the heart of both man and beast.

displayed both their names, just so there was no chance of a mistaken identity.

They were dubbed 'Beauty and the Beast' by the media. And after such a positive start, West Ham fans wondered if this unlikely pairing could lead the Hammers to a fairytale finish to the season.

Scoring Sensation

Dani's arrival – and the attendant explosion of publicity – had coincided with an upturn in fortunes at Upton Park. The relegation worries eased, though Redknapp started to voice concerns about his new wonderkid.

Dani was only 19 years old, living away

from his family for the first time. His agent sought to keep him busy by whisking him off to London nightspots, including a bizarre appearance on the red carpet for the premiere of *Twelve Monkeys* alongside Bruce Willis and Brad Pitt. Iain Dowie stayed at home, in case you were wondering.

They say being a top-class footballer is all about sacrifice. And as Dani adapted to his star status, he realised he would have to forego some aspects of his lifestyle. The first thing to get scrubbed off the list was training. Getting to Chadwell Heath for 10am was proving a real nuisance, especially when he'd been on the dancefloor until the early hours.

Plus, there was the effect that actually playing football was having on his energy levels. Despite his poor command of English, his use of the universal language had become legendary. He was linked romantically with a host of pop stars, TV hosts and glamour models. Keeping up with that sort of schedule wasn't conducive with 90 minutes of Premier League action.

West Ham stayed up; Dani's trousers stayed down. Redknapp lost patience, and the youngster's time in Claret and Blue was over almost as soon as it had started. He made only nine appearances.

The Show Must Go On

His career arc after east London was quite extraordinary. His next stop was Ajax. After all, when you're an ill-disciplined teenage superstar with too much money on your hands and a fondness for nocturnal activity, what better place to rehabilitate your career than Amsterdam?

Then there was a brief dalliance with Jose Mourinho at Benfica, possibly the

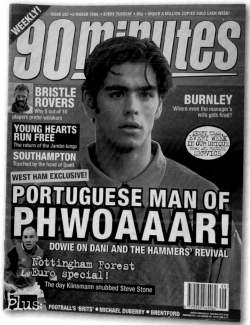

unlikeliest football partnership since Tony Adams first asked Caprice out for a drink. He lasted a mere five games.

His final outpost was Atletico Madrid, who were slumming it in Spain's second tier back then. It was now or never for the talented Portuguese to fulfil his potential. As ever, there were brief glimpses of his talent. He played a useful role in getting Atleti promoted, but the club decided not to renew his contract. Dani didn't argue. The physical requirements of being a professional athlete didn't really suit his idea of a work-life balance. Aged just 27, he retired on the spot.

These days, you can find him as a host on Portugal's version of *Strictly Come Dancing*, smiling at the camera whilst surrounded by the usual bevvy of scantily-clad beauties. You get the feeling that's what he wanted all along. Football just got in the way.

The Beautiful Game has been lit up by some extraordinary rivalries over the years: England v Germany, Real v Barcelona, and Richard Keys versus the accepted boundaries of good taste.

In the BBC commentary box, we were treated to a titanic battle between John Motson and Barry Davies. Motson was all hustle and bustle, Davies all poetry and prose. Listening to the latter in his pomp was astonishing. At times you'd forget he was there. He wasn't afraid to let the drama unfold on screen and say something only when absolutely necessary, which feels like a dagger through the heart of Steve McManaman's *raison d'etre*.

Here are three instances forever associated with one of the sport's most iconic voices. Three instances when you have to say... that was magnificent.

Tottenham v Arsenal, 1991

A year after the heroics of Italia 90, England was firmly in the grip of Gazzamania. Whilst the Spurs midfielder was busy writing new chapters in English football, the team as a whole were in the

midst of a familiar story: crap one week, great the next.

By April 1991 only the FA Cup offered escape from another dismal League campaign. And even then, ten of their starting eleven seemed to be doing their best to exit the competition early. Gascoigne was on a one-man mission to drag his team to the semi-final against their arch-rivals.

With only five minutes gone, Gazza stood over a free-kick. Davies, with the intuition of a man who'd seen the world's finest deliver in moments like these, could sense destiny looming:

> *Is Gascoigne going to have a crack? He is, you know. OH I SAY! BRILLIANT! That is Schoolboys' Own stuff. I bet even he can't believe it. Is there anything left from this man to surprise us?*

It's a line that still sends shivers down the spine of those who witnessed it live. The perfect description of the fairytale unfolding before our eyes: a boy living a dream, a boy living life to the fullest, and a boy unaware that life might never be this good again.

Argentina v Brazil, 1990

It's hard to find the words to describe Argentina's 1990 World Cup side. Four years is a long time in football. In 1986 Diego Maradona had the world at his feet. Even God – with a helping hand from Peter Shilton's concrete boots – was on his side. Now, one tournament cycle later, and the closest he got to Heaven was when he was high as a kite after a night on the marching powder.

The traditional term would be that Carlos Bilardo's side were a team 'in transition', which in football's unique vernacular is a polite way of saying they were a bunch of over-the-hill shithouses who arseholed their way magnificently to the semi-finals. Considering his face was known across the globe, Maradona had been almost anonymous during the group stages. His main contribution seemed to be rolling hysterically around the floor, screaming in agony, like a toddler that's just trodden on a Lego brick.

There was no finer example than the knockout game against arch-rivals Brazil. The Argentines were wretched from the first minute, battered from pillar to post. They spent the whole game not just chasing shadows but clinging to the oppo's shirts and trying to boot them into touch.

Then, with ten minutes to go, Maradona made his sole contribution to the game. Drifting past one man, then another, that peripheral vision of old returned for a split-second – and it was enough to win it:

> *This is Maradona. And he gets the ball through to Caniggiaaaaaaaaaa... SCORES! Taffarel looks at the ground. The Little Man has set up Argentina yet again.*

Long before Martin Tyler's AGUEEEEEEEEEEEEEEEEEEROOOO moment, this was perhaps the finest example of holding a single syllable for dramatic effect.

Holland v Argentina, 1998

On a sweltering night in Marseille, Argentina and Holland engaged in a titanic quarter-final that produced one of the finest goals in World Cup history. Whilst all around were losing their heads, the Iceman lived up to his reputation. A footballer's energy is his currency. And Bergkamp conserved his with the sort of vice-like grip that Margaret Thatcher reserved for welfare spending.

Whilst others wilted in the fiery French heat, the Dutchman waited for his moment. And it came with minutes to go. Frank De Boer sent a raking diagonal ball forward towards Bergkamp. His first touch was softer than a peck on your mum's cheek, the second sent Roberto Ayala out for a baguette and a packet of Gitanes, and the third curled the ball exquisitely past Carlos Roa:

> *Beautifully pulled down by Bergkamp. OH WHAT A GOAL! Dennis Bergkamp has won it for Holland! That was absolutely brilliant! From adversity to triumph for the Dutch. Those who were silent are now in song!*

Without the commentary, it's a fabulous finish.

With Davies's melodic scripture to accompany it, it actually heightens the on-screen action, playing a key part in some of football's most compelling theatre.

Once again, he'd found the perfect words for the perfect moment.

No one better managed the transition from the '80s to '90s than Sir Alex Ferguson. By December 1989, the writing seemed to be on the wall for Sir Alex at United; without a win in seven games, they found themselves drawn away in in the FA Cup to Brian Clough's high-flying Nottingham Forest. Similar poor form earlier in the season had seen the United fans unfurl a banner which read: "Three years of excuses and it's still crap... Ta-ra Fergie."

A defeat to Forest in January and, so the story goes, Ferguson was out of a job. In what was perhaps the most dramatic *Sliding Doors* moment of the entire '90s (aside from the actual film, *Sliding Doors*), Mark Robins nicked the only goal in a 1-0 win for United. Ferguson kept his job and the rest, as they say, is '90s football history. As written by a very dominant Scotsman.

However, Fergie's path to glory is paved with some of the biggest tear-ups this side of Frank Bruno. Sir Alex rattled, cajoled and wound up just about everyone in the game, but more often than not, his most tense and fiery missives were reserved for former friends and colleagues.

So, in no particular order, here's Fergie's most notorious fallings out.

Kevin Keegan
Perhaps the most famous Sir Alex fall-out of the '90s resulted in the live-TV nervous breakdown of rival Newcastle manager, Kevin Keegan.

A few weeks before Keegan shed himself of any composure whatsoever, Sir Alex Ferguson had complained that the likes of Leeds United and Nottingham Forest didn't try as hard against championship rivals Newcastle as they did against reigning champions Manchester United (which, to be fair, I would argue, is a fair point). This small aside stoked within

Keegan a fire that infamously, once appropriately stoked by Richard Keys and Andy Gray, blew up on Sky TV with the agitated exclamation, *"I'll tell you, honestly, I will love it if we beat them, love it!"* Needless to say, United went on to win the League that year.

Brian Kidd
It's easy to forget – what with everything that came after – that Brian Kidd is a *bona fide* Manchester United legend; and that legend was sealed on his 19th birthday as he scored in United's 4-1 win over Benfica in the 1968 European Cup final at Wembley, in just his second season as a professional footballer.

Fast-forward 20 years and Kidd found himself somewhat in the footballing wilderness – until Sir Alex picked up the phone and offered Kidd a community

> *They're down? They needed a win tonight? I thought they needed a point.*

role, scouting and coaching young players. What happened next is the stuff of legend. Kidd assumed that youth role at United at the precise moment a generation-defining collection of talent started coming through; from Giggs to Scholes, Brian Kidd was on hand to lay the foundations for United's decade of triumphs, which promptly followed at a relentless pace.

The most iconic moment of that early success came as Brian Kidd fell to his knees and pumped his hands toward the sky as United sealed the Premier League in 1993, but there was also the Double a year later and again in 1996, before another title in 1997.

But come 1998, Kidd, no doubt

justifiably confident in his own abilities, was willing to approach that most criminal sin as Sir Alex's assistant and go into management himself. Kidd joined Blackburn Rovers in December 1998 and promptly spent £20 million on a raft of players who were, for want of a better term, useless. Ashley Ward for £4.5 million from Barnsley, Matt Jansen for £4.1 million from Crystal Palace and Jason McAteer at £4 million from Liverpool proved to be expensive follies as Kidd's Blackburn lurched toward a relegation that was to come just four years after they'd been crowned champions.

And when relegation was to be confirmed, who was there to make it a certainty with a 0-0 draw but Sir Alex Ferguson and the United team Kidd had left five months previously. Most hilariously, Sir Alex fired shots at Kidd in the post-match interview by claiming to have been absolutely clueless about the fact he'd relegated his former assistant: *"They're down? They needed a win tonight? I thought they needed a point,"* claimed Fergie, tongue suspiciously in cheek.

More vitriol was to be spilled when Ferguson's autobiography, *Managing My Life*, was published later that summer. Fergie used

the book as a vehicle to ridicule Kidd's insistence that United not sign Dwight Yorke ahead of John Hartson, before going on to state that Kidd was both a 'complex' and 'insecure' person. Kidd in turn suggested that *"Walt Disney are trying to buy the film rights to his book as a sequel to* Fantasia.*"*

Happily, they're back on speaking terms now and were even known to share the traditional post-match bottle or two of wine toward the end of Ferguson's career.

David Beckham
There's a strong argument that Beckham was the footballing man of the '90s, the supporting evidence lying in the haul of trophies he was able to take back to the red half of Manchester: six Premier League titles, two FA Cups, four Charity Shields and, of course, that Champions' League trophy won most famously in 1999. However, while Becks was the golden boy of this era, it's worth recounting how that famous relationship turned to absolute shit. Firstly, Ferguson

suffered real discomfort at the fact that Beckham was becoming more pop-culture icon than footballer. His relationship with Posh Spice didn't help; during their early courtship, Becks flew to Ireland to see Posh without telling Fergie. When

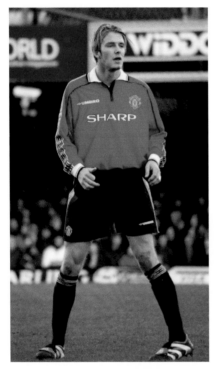

Ferguson saw him in the airport, he blanked him: *"I was coming back at 6am for training, I was sat in the lounge and the manager walked in. He didn't talk to me. I knew I was in a little bit of trouble,"* Becks would later tell BBC Radio.

The frequent hairstyle changes did nothing to please Fergie either. Beckham famously shaved his head with a view to unveiling it during a fixture away to Leicester. Becks wore a beanie hat in the warm-up to build the suspense. This too infuriated his boss.

Four years after Beckham's greatest triumph for United, in February 2003, Ferguson prepared some infamous, post-match hairdryer treatment for his team that had just lost to rivals Arsenal 2-0 at home in the FA Cup. Bang in the centre of his target was Beckham, and Beckham was having none of it.

Fergie explained what happened next in his autobiography: *"He was around 12 feet from me. Between us on the floor lay a row of boots. David swore. I moved towards him, and as I approached I kicked a boot. It hit him right above the eye. Of course, he rose to have a go at me and the players stopped him. 'Sit down,' I said. 'You've let your team down. You can argue as much as you like.'"*

The next day, Beckham drove to training with surgical tape plastered all over his eyebrow, but the wound would never truly heal. By the summer, like so many who had crossed Fergie before, he was out. Flogged to Real Madrid for £24.5 million. *"I had no aspirations to leave United,"* said Becks. *"There was never any revenge. I was hurt and angry at the time at how the situation had gone because throughout the season I was left out of certain games but never thought it would lead to me leaving."*

The Space-Time Continuum

It's there on the touchline that we see perhaps the most iconic image of Sir Alex Ferguson. The one indelibly ingrained in the psyche of anyone who loved '90s football: that of our protagonist, red faced and furious, tapping his watch like a maniac. Because it often felt that Sir Alex's most violent fury was focussed on the nature of TIME ITSELF.

Tapping at his timepiece to end a match, tapping to extend it. The space-time continuum, no doubt petrified at whatever it had done to displease The Scottish One, seemed to bend to his will whenever he wished, in a phenomenon that came to be known as 'Fergie Time'. And never was this more evident than when they won their first Premier League title in 1993.

Still without a League title since the '60s, United played Sheffield Wednesday in April 1993. Lying second in the table with five minutes to go, they found themselves 1-0 down at home. Out of nowhere, an unlikely goalscoring hero in Steve Bruce netted an equaliser. Looking on from the goalpost of the goal he was supposed to be defending, Nigel Worthington's face unmistakably said, "all of this is a bit of an inconvenience."

And then, with a completely absurd 97 minutes on the clock, Bruce scored again to put United top and on course for their

He said, 'There's only one guv'nor around here, Incey – and it ain't you.'

first Premier League title. Unabashed ecstasy followed on the United bench; particularly from assistant Brian Kidd, who legged it on to the pitch and exposed his midriff three times in ten seconds as he punched the air and dropped to his knees with a joy rarely expressed in physical form among actual adults.

Time had been challenged by Sir Alex and it wilted pathetically, in just the way Nigel Worthington defends from corners.

Paul Ince
You've got to respect a footballer who turns up at a new club, especially one the size of United, and requests to be called 'The Guv'nor'. Ince's alibi for having the nickname is suspect to say the least. At various points, he's attributed it to his East

London snooker-hall mates and Brian Kidd, but perhaps the most believable version of events comes via Steve Bruce who suggested Ince invented it himself: *"It just showed you how much front and bottle he had to be called 'the Guv'nor' even when he first walked in the door. I just thought: 'Who's this cocky little thing from West Ham?'"*

Ince cemented the nickname with a private number plate in his playing days that read 'GUV 8'; and with a manager in Ferguson not known for players who don't seem to understand the pecking order, a clash was inevitable.

Ince would later recall the bad taste left in his mouth when he was lambasted for giving the ball away in the dying embers of a game they were winning 3-1: *"He starts coming up to me in my face and I'm thinking, I'm not having this. So I stand up, we are face to face and he is shouting, and as he is shouting I've got spit going in my eye. I'm trying to talk back to him but every time I open my mouth the spit goes in so I thought I would keep my mouth shut."*

The two still weren't on speaking terms the following week, as the battle for dominance continued. As Incey would later tell TalkSport: *"We played head tennis on the Thursday and he was the referee. It gets to 9-9, Steve Bruce heads the ball up in the air and I do an overhead kick, it hits the line to win the game.*

"Sir Alex goes: 'Out'.

"Because we weren't speaking at the time I could not say anything. I looked at him, he said, 'Out, game over, they won'.

"As I walked away, he said, 'There's only one guv'nor around here, Incey – and it ain't you."

Despite delivering for United two League titles, two FA Cups, a European Cup Winners' Cup and a European Super Cup in six years, Fergie called time on their turbulent relationship in 1995 – although the exact breaking point is the subject of much debate.

The favoured theory for the parting belongs to Ferguson biographer Frank Worrall, who attributes Ince's infamous nickname as the final straw. The story goes that, toward the end of Ince's United career, he arrived at Old Trafford at the same time as Ferguson, and the door staff welcomed only one of the two as 'the Guv'nor'; obviously, much to Fergie's fury, it wasn't the Scotsman.

However, the feud really blew up a few years later when Ince (then at Liverpool) prepared to face off with United, Ferguson's pep-talk for the encounter being captured for an ITV documentary, *The Alex Ferguson Story*: *"You just make sure you're ready for Ince tomorrow... He's a f**king big-time Charlie."* Fergie even went on to describe Ince as a 'bottler'.

However, years passed and Ferguson would later express his regrets about both the documentary and his comments. *"We let a camera into our dressing room, which we had never done before, and it won't happen again. It wasn't a personality issue with Paul,"* he later conceded.

"With Paul you could not have a honeymoon all the time, because he was such a volatile character, but he never let us down."

Almost the Entire UK Media

Ferguson has, at one point or another, fallen out with almost every single aspect of the British news meda; from outlets to broadcasters, no one was safe. In 2005, he even fell out with the club's own official TV channel after a presenter opined that 4-4-2 might be a better formation than Ferguson's preferred 4-5-1 – a suggestion that resulted in a furious Ferguson boycott.

Sometimes, Ferguson would fall out with broadcasters without them even knowing what they'd done wrong. Robbie Savage once revealed that, despite being neighbours with Sir Alex for six months, the Scot had blanked him at every turn for some unknown slight that Savage was never able to discern.

Chief among Ferguson's most publicised media feuds was the seven years he spent not talking to the BBC, after a documentary called *Father and Son* alluded to his son, Jason Ferguson, potentially exploiting his father's influence in his job as a football agent. In some respect, his Beeb ban had preceded the documentary incident by more than a decade with Fergie refusing to talk to BBC Radio 5's Alan Green since 1992 for another separate grievance.

Gary Lineker provoked Fergie's wrath by suggesting that Ferguson's years-long, drawn-out grudge was 'childish'. Sir Alex replied with a petulant 'I know you are! So what am I?' statement that was almost straight out of the playground: *"Gary Lineker – a bright boy from the BBC – says I'm childish. Well, he should know about that himself. He's been subjected to a lot of stuff in the media himself and he's had stuff stopped from getting in newspapers from time to time.*

"So he'll understand what childishness means, because he is childish. I don't think I'm childish at all."

Ferguson's *modus operandi* was once famously, and accidentally, captured in a press conference by a live microphone the Scot hadn't noticed.

After an Associated Press journalist asked a question about Ryan Giggs that Fergie didn't like, he was heard to say: *"We'll get him. Ban him on Friday."*

Sky later broadcast that footage, and guess what? They got a ban from Old Trafford, too.

Cynics amongst you might suggest they'd be even harder to save with Massimo Taibi in goal.

Long before fans of the modern era found themselves scrutinising their teams via their progress through the Asia Trophy – or a similar cynically made-up international tournament – there was only one way to figure out if your team was about to start the season with a misplaced confidence unseen since Apollo Creed entered the ring at the start of *Rocky IV*. Good old friendlies.

Anyone who's ever been to a friendly knows they occupy a bizarre, netherworldy space somewhere between watching a game in a park and an early-season League Cup tie. Friendlies retain all the trappings of an actual game of football (the players, the trip to the ground, the half-time pint) but without any jeopardy, fear of failure or, indeed, point.

As with most things in life, it's difficult to shake off your prejudices when your lived experience provides you with an ample amount of ammunition to say "this is rubbish." So when it comes to friendlies, even now, I find myself unable to reach any other conclusion than they serve almost no purpose.

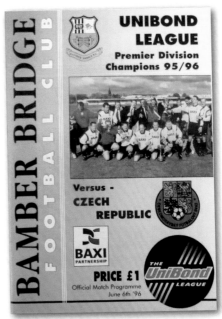

Oxford City v West Ham, 1994

Perhaps I say friendlies are pointless for one specific reason. West Ham, in the '90s, treated friendlies with a disrespect rarely seen throughout all professional sport.

One shining example of this utter lack of regard for the pre-season kickaround was the time we played away, one summer's night, at Oxford City and played an actual fan in the second half – the reason being that he'd given manager Harry Redknapp so much gip in the first.

And in a further sign that these games mean absolutely nothing, that fan (a bloke named Steve) actually put the ball in the net! (Although, in defence of the Oxford defence, it was later ruled out for offside).

> *The 2,300 fans in attendance that day witnessed an entire country maul their local heroes 9-1.*

But it wasn't just West Ham who had scant regard for these warm-up games, occasionally it was entire countries.

Bamber Bridge v Czech Republic, 1996

The Czech Republic's preparation for Euro 96 was quite simply astonishing. Weeks before Karel Poborsky and his team-mates were to impress their way to the final, they found themselves testing their mettle not against other nations, but instead Bamber Bridge (population: 12,126).

The 2,300 fans in attendance that day (almost 20 per cent of the village) witnessed an entire country maul their local heroes 9-1 in a game from which it was surely impossible to extract any meaning whatsoever. In fact, attempting to derive any meaning from pre-season games is as difficult as unpicking the decision to destroy any suspense in *Rocky IV* by putting a picture of Rocky's victory over Ivan Drago on the actual movie poster advertising the film.

But the Czech Republic wasn't the only entire actual country that was prepared to take on all sorts, however inconsequential, in a worthless friendly.

Leyton Orient v Wales, 1996

Back in the mid '90s, Bobby Gould had been handed the reins at Wales. And as they prepared to take on the whipping boys of international football, San Marino, Gouldy decided he'd experiment with a different tactic, playing preparatory games against yet further inferior opposition.

The plan began well with the Welsh nation (population: 3.136 million) beating the Welsh town of Cwmbran (population: 48,535) 6-1. Up next, Gould looked to a team fourth from bottom of the old English Third Division (League Two in the new money) to provide a test for the likes of global footballing icon Ryan Giggs and co. The end result was a 2-1 victory for Orient that must surely go down as one of the most embarrassing incidents in the Welsh FA's 144-year history.

Football now is a meal prepared by expert chefs who carefully consider each ingredient months, sometimes years in advance. Gone are the days of 'on the hoof' friendly games and any accompanying rank amateurishness.

Anyone who may have seen Manchester City's Amazon Prime documentary will no doubt have drawn similarities between their remarkable training facilities and those of Ivan Drago's; the high-tech

muscle machines, clever people walking around with clipboards, the glassy-eyed professionalism of athletes who know nothing but winning every week. And the associate professionalism of football administrators who at least vaguely seem like they have a plan.

But the truth is sport, much like the decision to have a picture of Rocky beating Ivan Drago on the poster of *Rocky IV*, is a nonsense.

We can pretend to ourselves that all

the right preparation – having the right kind of pre-season and other-worldly training facilities – is capable of producing a ruthlessly efficient level of sporting performance incapable of losing; but it simply cannot, as Rocky himself showed us time and again.

The game may have changed substantially since the '90s... "But if I can change, and you can change, everybody can change!"

There are so many curiosities of English matchday culture in the '90s that are rarely talked about. Let me venture a few: the seats at the old Wembley stadium didn't have any backs to them. Every football ground smelled of cigarette and cigar smoke and – despite never being a smoker myself – I associate that awful smell with pleasant memories. The printed football fanzine was of huge importance, now sadly declined in the internet age. And what about going into a ground and ringing your mate on your brick-like mobile phone, so you can wave at each other for no reason whatsoever?

On one occasion in the mid '90s when West Ham played Chelsea, my dad did just that; pulled out his new, chunky mobile to ring his mate in the away end, literally just to wave at one other. I remember my blood turning cold as I realised, shockingly, that people sat around me would know our family had ties to the enemy.

Another aspect of the matchday experience now sadly consigned to history would be paper season-ticket books. As a season-ticket holder in the '90s, chances were you would excitedly receive your book over the summer and, in time, take it to your local football stadium where a number would be displayed above your entry gate – a notification for you to remove the corresponding paper ticket and hand it over to one of the grim souls locked into the turnstile, who would then admit you to the game.

Those ticket books were eventually replaced at most grounds by plastic cards, nowhere near as thrilling as their paper counterparts. The plastic revolution has also led to the demise of one of the most popular footballing protests of the '90s; the tearing up of the season ticket!

It usually worked like this. Around the end of the season, when all hope had been lost, a fuming supporter would rush on to the pitch and, in the best Shakespearean overacting he could muster, tear up his paper season-ticket book mere feet from an often glum manager who would pretend not to see it. However, I always thought it was a curiosity of such season-ticket ripping protests that they never seemed to happen before spring. In fact, it was almost always the last or penultimate game of the season, when the season ticket was almost obsolete in any case. A fact which, lets face it, undermined any fury our theatrical supporter could gather.

Another aspect of the '90s football fandom experience, for a certain generation, now sadly lost to the cynicism and worldweariness of age, is the childlike

thrill that would accompany a trip to another football ground for the first time. More often than not, as an away fan in the away end. Occasionally, as an impartial observer in the home end. But also, very rarely, observing the away team as a secret agent, in the home end.

Remember the first time you pulled off such an act of treachery? If you've got this far through the book, there's a good chance it happened in the '90s. At this point, I should probably rattle through the rules for away fans in the home end.

Firstly, and most obviously, there is to be no jumping up and cheering when your team scores. However, it's this most vital

Remember the first time you observed the away team as a secret agent in the home end?

rule that feels most unnatural: watching your team score, and not reacting, takes a kind of discipline rarely exhibited outside of Tibetan monasteries. It goes against every natural impulse. But if you want to get out of enemy territory alive, without detection, it's the only course of action at your disposal. In my experience, grabbing your mate's thigh works quite well, or alternatively, try channelling your excitement through a stand-up, *faux* raging at the home team's defending.

The other rules, still observed to this day, include not loudly talking about "us" in reference to the away team, "you" in reference to the home team or sharing any expert-level intelligence on the away team at an audible level (eg "Can you believe we signed Gary McAllister in the summer on

a Bosman? He really does represent terrific value"). If you manage all that, you'll generally get in and out of the ground in one piece in any era.

Of course, football grounds are now much better than they were in the '90s. You'll do well to find one in an intensely residentially packed, urban area. You'll rarely see a ground with four stands in four different styles from four completely different eras; in fact, I can't even think of a stadium now that has a supermarket for a stand (RIP Burnden Park).

The new Wembley has backs to its seats. Bolton have four stands that look the same. There is no smoking in stadiums (probably a good thing that, to be fair). No one rings their mates to wave, the matchday food is edible these days, and you can't tear up a plastic season-ticket card (unless you're blessed with a freakish strength the likes of which this country hasn't seen since Geoff Capes).

Yes, the '90s are over; but sometimes you can rip the back off a plastic seat and pretend you're still there.

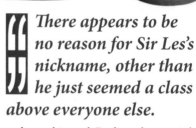

Why don't football players have colourful, amusing, unique, stupid, slanderous, patronising or punful nicknames any more? Is 'The HurriKane' really the best the 21st century can do? When it came to player nicknames, you might be able to guess which decade had all the best ones sewn up...

'Sicknote' aka Darren Anderton

Darren Anderton's style was bewildering; he was languid yet pacy, leggy yet skilful and somehow underpowered yet capable of incredible long-range goals. In 1995, Anderton's goal for England against Sweden spawned endless schoolboy attempts to recreate it in the garden or up the park. All doomed. Struck from outside the box, it sensationally ricocheted off both posts, in the blink of an eye, before going in.

However, most notable among Anderton's many achievements is his nickname: 'Sicknote'. It's fair to say he suffered more than a few injuries over his 18-year career, but the signs were there within his first two years as a pro when Portsmouth goalkeeper Andy Gosney came out with a bit of banter that's still going strong 30 years later; football was the game, and 'Sicknote' became the name. Anderton played 30 times for England and amassed 471 League games, but perhaps remains just as well known for all the other ones he missed through injury.

'Sir Les' aka Les Ferdinand

There appears to be no reason for Sir Les's nickname other than the fact he just seemed a class above everyone else, even

> **There appears to be no reason for Sir Les's nickname, other than he just seemed a class above everyone else.**

perhaps a bit regal. Ferdinand cemented his knight-like reputation on Tyneside, netting 48 goals in two enormously successful seasons for Newcastle United from 1995 to 1997; and it was here in the North East that the sophisticated nickname really took hold.

I also think it's fair to say Sir Les enjoyed the moniker somewhat, given that he went so far as to give his 1997 autobiography the title of *Sir Les*. Skip on a few years, and in 2005 Ferdinand officially became Les Ferdinand MBE; so it would seem the authorities are quite rightly chipping away at the administrative formalities necessary to make 'Sir Les' something more than an affectionate sobriquet.

'The Terminator' aka Julian Dicks

Known for a lack of discipline that struck fear into opponents, fans saw fit to bestow Julian Dicks with a nickname that drew allusions to another bloke with a total insensitivity to both pain and empathy.

Whereas the Terminator had been sent back in time from 2029 to kill the mother of a future resistance leader, Julian Dicks had been sent to East London for £300k from Birmingham City with the express instruction from manager John Lyall to "get a bit physical". Needless to say, the Hammers' Bristol-born 'Terminator' more than over-delivered on this brief, with Dicks developing a tough-tackling style that might even have made Skynet blush.

'Batigol' aka Gabriel Batistuta

Argentina's all-time leading goalscorer until the advent of a Mr Messi, Batistuta is best known for his mesmeric nine-year spell with Fiorentina, who in turn gave him the nickname he still commands in Florence to this day.

"Why does he have this nickname?" I hear you cry. Well *battere* in Italian means to batter or beat. And *gol* means, derrr, 'goal'. So the nickname is basically a play on his surname, but can also be interpreted as 'battering in goals'. Goals which were frequently followed up his iconic, double clenched-fist celebration, so iconic that it has been immortalised in statue form in his native Argentina. This statue is substantially better than the one Fiorentina fans hastily erected in bronze, which looks uncannily like Oliver Cromwell holding a corner flag.

'The Animal' aka Edmundo

In Brazil, Edmundo became so synonymous with incidents of ill-discipline and controversy and that only one nickname seemed to speak to his seeming lack of humanity. In a career littered with near-feral and occasionally carnal incidents, one example from his Fiorentina days sums up his priorities. In 1999, with his team top of the league, and Batigol injured, 'The Animal' decided to eschew the title race to fly back to Brazil for the Rio carnival purely for the purpose of partying; needless to say, he burned his bridges with the fans, his team-mates and manager Giovanni Trapattoni.

Such indiscretions were comfortably trumped the time he hired an entire circus to perform in his back garden for his son's first birthday. The show complete, 'The Animal' ratcheted up the afterparty by getting leathered on beer and whiskey with Pedrinho, one of the performers. Of course, there would be nothing wrong with that, except for the small matter of Pedrinho being a chimpanzee.

UNFORGETTABLES

JULIAN DICKS

FRANCE 98

EDMUNDO

BRASIL

Golden goal was always a bit of nonsense, but the '90s were a hotbed for flights of fancy fiddling with the game's laws and traditions. Quite a few innovations stuck – players' names on shirts, huge squad numbers and not drinking 50 pints the night before a game – but other bright-spark innovations turned into absolute farce.

One such travesty occurred as a consequence of a seemingly innocent rule-change experiment, where the 1994 Caribbean Cup qualifiers were used as a testing ground.

The qualifiers were to be decided via round-robin groups of three teams. But peculiarly, the organisers had decided that every single game had to have a winner; if a match were tied after 90 minutes, it was to be decided in extra time via a golden goal, or ultimately on penalties. But then another little tweak was floated on top: if a team scored a golden goal, it would count twice. So a golden goal scored at 0-0 would result in a final score of 2-0 for the team who scored the single winner. Good clean fun. What could possibly go wrong?

Cut now to the final group game in the qualifiers, Barbados v Grenada. The countries' standings ahead of the kick-off were as follows:

Team	Pld	W	D	L	GF	GA	GD	Pts
Grenada	1	1	0	0	2	0	+2	3
Puerto Rico	2	1	0	1	1	2	-1	3
Barbados	1	0	0	1	0	1	-1	0

As you can see, the home team Barbados could still qualify in first position, but only if they won by a clear two-goal margin. And by the 83rd minute, Barbados were on course for a 2-0 victory; until, that is,

Grenada went and nicked one back. 2-1.

The game dragged on, Barbados desperately needing another to go through. With nerves setting in, the game approached the 87th minute when someone had a brainwave – if Barbados now scored an own goal to tie the game 2-2, they would force the tie into extra time. Using this cunning plan, they could give themselves another 30 minutes to score a single goal, which would count double, and take them through.

> *In the 87th minute someone had a brainwave – if Barbados scored an own goal, they would force the tie into extra time.*

What happened next is one of the most '90s moments of '90s football. Barbadian defender Terry Sealey dribbled the ball back to his goalkeeper, played a coy little one-two, stopped, thought for a second, then absolutely leathered it into his own net. 2-2.

The Grenadian players at this point twigged what was happening. And then, stunningly, realised that another course of action, one even more extraordinary than what they'd just witnessed, was available to them – as now either a 3-2 defeat or a 3-2 win would be enough to take them through. In practice, this meant they had two minutes plus injury time to score a goal IN EITHER NET. And therefore Barbados were faced with the insane prospect of having to defend BOTH goals until extra time ticked around.

In short, Barbados defended for their lives (strikers defending the opposition goal, while defenders defended their goal), and somehow the 90 minutes finished 2-2. Those stunning few minutes were only witnessed by those present; but how on earth did Grenada manage to fail to score an own goal when they had the kick-off after the goal? Grenada's manager James Clarkson said after the match: "Our players did not even know which direction to attack: our goal or their goal!" Which at least goes some way to explaining how they failed to do either.

But also, how did Barbados do the defending? Split into teams of five and run at each goal?

In the end, Barbados, who set these crazy wheels in motion, did get their golden goal to set a final score of 4-2 and send them through to the 1994 Caribbean Cup. Their genius had sent Grenada packing. But

> *How did Barbados do the defending? Split into teams of five and run at each goal?*

final word to Grenada's losing manager and these crazy rule changes that were a product of their time: "The person who came up with these rules must be a candidate for a madhouse..."

Ladies and gentlemen, the '90s.

One of the most remarkable aspects of England's World Cup campaign in 1998 was the sheer drama around the squad selection. Undecided on the mere 22 players he would be taking to France 98, England manager Glenn Hoddle, two years into the job, imagined he could manoeuvre himself around the quandary by picking a larger squad of 28 and then whittling it down via a pre-tournament training camp.

It was a move that the *X-Factor* generation might more easily understand as 'judges' houses'.

While the logic apparently made perfect sense, Hoddle, still young for an England boss at 40 and inexperienced on the international stage, had set an explosive trap for himself; specifically, when the time came to inform six England players it was time to leave, and even more specifically, when one of those six had the temperament of Paul Gascoigne.

But, winding the clock back just over a month before that chaotic afternoon in the hotel rooms of La Manga, Hoddle went about ratcheting up the selection pressure further than ever before with his decision to hold an England B international at Loftus Road against Russia. Unhappy with the traditional system of England friendlies from which to judge the prowess of his players, Hoddle decided that another route was open to him. He would request that players in contention for the squad perform for him, in what was effectively a beauty parade, under the banner of England B for a chance to make it to the A team.

In Hoddle's defence, England B games weren't a phenomenon unique to him. Terry Venables had held two in 1994 and his predecessors Bryan Robson and Graham Taylor had both held a few. But somehow, looking back, the unedifying spectacle that preceded England's squad announcement in May 1998 and this particular match – England B v Russia a month prior – feel intrinsically linked to the ego of one man. A man who, like some '90s Middlesex-born Julius Caesar, wanted a group of men to do battle at the Colosseum on Loftus Road, so he could lift his thumb or otherwise to their international ambitions.

Into this scene, step forward the most renowned talent on the South Coast since Benny Hill, a man known simply as 'Le God', Southampton's finest – Matthew Paul Le Tissier. Le Tiss was perhaps every bit the talent Paul Gascoigne was in all but one department; Matt had all the pace of a turning P&O ferry. One aspect of his professionalism most suspect was his diet which was, for want of a better phrase, an absolute disgrace.

Cramping up with stomach aches during a training session in his early '90s pomp, the physio pressed him, "What did you have for breakfast Matt?" To which Le God replied, "Two double sausage and egg McMuffins". The physio, no doubt aghast, cautioned against two in future, but knowing Matt's penchant for them

Instead of beating players with quick acceleration, Le Tissier would befuddle them with his close control.

and seemingly having a similar disregard for nutrition, thought one would probably be okay.

Matthew Le Tissier compensated for his sloth-like pace and slovenly diet with a natural ability that marked him out as one of the most skilful of his generation. Instead of beating players with quick acceleration, he'd befuddle them with his close control, frequently and delicately lifting the ball over their heads and, more often than not, leaving top-flight defences on their backsides. Another tactic Le Tissier would deploy in lieu of speed was as simple as it was spectacular: he'd just

leather the ball into the top corner of the net from 40 yards to save himself from all that running.

The end result was endless Goal of the Month competitions dominated by arguably the greatest player in the history of the Saints. Such was his innate ability that when Alan Ball arrived at relegation-threatened Southampton in January 1994 he proposed a simple new tactic to the team: give the ball to Le Tiss. In those last 16 games of the 1993/94 season under Ball, he scored 15 times as Southampton survived relegation by a point.

But unlike Alan Ball, one man who wouldn't be winning a World Cup with England or building a team around Le Tiss was Glenn Hoddle. Unless of course, Matt could prove the doubters wrong whilst wearing the captain's armband as England B took on Russia on 21st April 1998.

The team lined up on the night without Chris Sutton, who'd previously informed

Glenn Hoddle that he wouldn't be playing as "he didn't do rehearsals" (he never played for England again). Up for the game, however, was our hero Matt Le Tissier. Thirty years old and no doubt well aware that summer's World Cup was his last chance to shine on the world stage.

The match starts and, two minutes in, Le Tiss hooks a cross in from the right hand side of the pitch with his left peg; Sir Les Ferdinand connects with his head and England go 1-0 up. No doubt Hoddle already has something to think about.

Eleven minutes later and the plot begins to thicken as England play a loose cross into the box. It flies over the defender's head and ahead of our hero's foot on the half volley. It's 2-0 to England B.

The score then stays static until Russia fire one back on the 83rd minute. Which surely annoys Le Tiss, who promptly runs up the other end, juggles the ball between his feet and betwixt two Russian defenders before rifling it into the bottom corner.

"He looks trim, he looks sharp," says Hoddle's predecessor Terry Venables of the goal.

"He's so casual in the way he takes his chance!" effuses Bob Wilson.

With the clock running down, another loose ball finds its way powered into the box. Le Tiss trots in, controls it with his right, smashes it in with his left; two touches. 4-1 England B. A hat-trick, an assist. A performance thats almost comical for its brilliance. Yet while the fans at Loftus Road cheered on Le Tiss's third of the night, one man had left early to beat the traffic. Sadly, that man was the only one who really mattered.

The truly absurd thing about that evening is that it wasn't even enough to see Le Tissier through to Hoddle's long-list 28 man squad. It was Le Tissier's last game in an England shirt. It was a Roy of the Rovers-esque performance, but for Hoddle, it wasn't enough.

Matt held the grudge against Hoddle for the rest of his career, including a brief spell when both were at Southampton together in the 2000/01 season and another when they were briefly in the same restaurant, exchanging an awkward 'hello'. In the years after, Le Tiss would speculate that Hoddle's snub was payback for his snub on a move to Chelsea, years prior. Whatever the case, and however good Hoddle may have been as a coach, it's his man-management skills (or lack of them) that were to draw most ire as he continued to whittle down his squad for France 1998.

Long after 1998, Teddy Sheringham would be effusive in his praise for Glenn Hoddle the player: "He was so graceful. The ball would come over and he would catch it on his back, knock it up and volley it back to where it came from. Everything he did was so classy." But less effusive in his praise for Hoddle the manager: "Then when I met him man to man, it was, 'Oh my God, what a c**t.'"

Whereas Terry Venables had fostered

sensational squad morale with a laid-back approach, Glenn Hoddle arrived with an approach seemingly inspired by two '90s cult classics; somewhere between *The Demon Headmaster* and *The Brittas Empire*. His central philosophy seemed to be that players weren't to be trusted.

As future England manager Gareth Southgate was to say of him: "Deep down, I believe, he is a decent person, but he doesn't communicate well with people and he has a way of rubbing players up the wrong way."

31st May 1998, La Manga Club, Cartagena, Spain. Hoddle has lined up 28 appointments in his room for each member of his squad to learn their fate. He intends to tell them all face to face, man to man; it's what he believes is the right thing to do. Five of the six cut that day barely make the headlines. Ian Walker of Spurs,

No one drank as much as Gascoigne that night, and no one else finished the evening in the hotel swimming pool, either.

Andy Hinchcliffe of Sheffield Wednesday, Dion Dublin of Coventry and Nicky Butt and Phil Neville of Manchester United. Gary Neville later described his brother as being utterly distraught; Phil himself would go on to describe it as his worst moment in football.

But it's Gazza's demise, far more than that of Le Tissier, for which the pre-World Cup 1998 cull is best remembered. Paul Gascoigne, who had thrilled for England at Italia 90 and dazzled at Euro 96, could sense trouble. Hoddle had given the team a rare night off before the squad

announcement the day after. No one drank as much as Gascoigne that night, and no one else finished the evening in the hotel swimming pool, either.

While Gascoigne paced the hall nervously the following day, waiting for his appointment with Hoddle, he came across his old friend and former Newcastle colleague – now the England coach under Hoddle – Glenn Roeder. Roeder had tears in his eyes and Gazza knew they were for him. He kicked down the door to Hoddle's room while Phil Neville received his own bad news; by all accounts, bedlam followed at the realisation of Gazza's worst fears. He was out.

It's hard to look beyond the France 1998 tournament as anything other than a tragedy for that generation of England players. The snub of Le Tissier was one thing, but the denial of Gazza just seemed cruel. If you watch post-match the footage after England lose to West Germany on penalties at the semi-final of Italia 90, you'll see England manager Bryan Robson console a young Gazza with the words, "Don't worry, you're young, this won't be your last World Cup." Sadly, it was; but it was still one more World Cup than Le Tissier ever made it to.

The World Cup of 1998 ended with a loss on penalties to Argentina and a betrayal narrative that saw future captain David Beckham offered up as a patsy. Glenn Hoddle survived another six months, before an interview with *The Times* revealed some, frankly, awful views on what disabled people may have done in past lives to deserve their fate.

However, the piece that sealed Hoddle's fate concluded with two sentences that offer a poetic footnote to the whole affair: "You have to look at things that happened in your life and ask 'why?' It comes around."

Ruud Gullit may have coined the phrase, but in terms of its actual physical manifestation, no one personified 'sexy football' better than David Ginola.

The free-spirited Frenchman arrived from PSG for £2.5 million in the summer of 1995 after rebuffing the advances of Johan Cruyff's Barcelona. Kevin Keegan's romantic vision of Newcastle United and balls-to-the-wall attacking football felt like the perfect location for his next adventure.

His arrival caused hearts to flutter amongst Newcastle's female fanbase. With his movie-star looks, Ginola was unlike anything they'd ever seen before. He became an instant heartthrob, certainly a significant upgrade on Jimmy Nail.

And when he put his boots on, he soon earned the adulation of the Toon terraces. The beauty of Ginola was his unapologetic disinterest in the actual match itself. The football pitch was his playground, a stage for him to showcase his full repertoire of flicks and tricks. If his team won a few points along the way, then *très bien*. He was here to bring some Gallic flair to the Gallowgate End. And they loved him for it.

For 18 months Ginola was at the heart of one of the most enthralling teams of the Premier League era, scoring a handful of sensational goals then relaxing with a cigarette in the dressing room afterwards. But when King Kev abruptly resigned in February 1997, the love affair was over. New boss Kenny Dalglish was far less enamoured than his predecessor with his French winger. Compared to Keegan, the Scot had the positivity of a professional pall-bearer. The court of Dalglish had no need for a jester like Ginola.

Which is how the dashing David found himself en route to another of English football's most romantic outposts: White Hart Lane. Spurs had long since

> **His arrival caused hearts to flutter amongst Newcastle's female fanbase.**

ceased buying silver polish, so their only expectation on a Saturday afternoon was to be entertained. Once again, Ginola had found a spiritual home.

Unfortunately, his new boss Gerry Francis didn't last long. And the next appointment wasn't really to Ginola's taste. Enter another hard-nosed Scotsman, George Graham. The dour dictator took an instant dislike to his team's left-sided luxury. Too much artistry, not enough arsehole. Much to his manager's disdain, tracking back and tackling were not high on the list of Ginola's preferred Saturday afternoon activities.

It left Graham in a quandary. His Arsenal

affiliations meant he was about as popular on the Tottenham terraces as a chunk of Kryptonite in Superman's jockstrap. Dropping Ginola would cause civil unrest amongst the North London natives. So, the two existed in a marriage of inconvenience for the duration of their time together.

It was a union that yielded success for both. A League Cup win kept Graham's many detractors at bay, whilst Ginola added PFA Player of the Year and FWA Footballer of the Year in 1998/99 to his own personal accolades.

Not that anyone remembers, really. Mention the name Ginola and people think about the long-range goals and the L'Oreal hair. A player who dazzled and danced across the land. And refused to ever change his principles on the Beautiful Game. Because he was worth it.

The year is 1991 and in an Essex soap factory we find amateur footballer and future West Ham and Charlton legend, Steve Jones, hard at work. The soap factory was Steve's day job, a regular Monday-to-Friday, nine-to-five gig. A workplace comparable to that of many fans who filled football grounds across the country every week. However, in Steve's early-'90s spare time, he was also one of the most prolific non-league strikers in the semi-professional Isthmian League, scoring at a rate which would make Messi blush, at 120 goals in 70-odd games.

With Steve firing at this rate in the non-league, a few big clubs started sniffing around. First Dave Bassett's Sheffield United asked for a trial, then hesitated. Meanwhile, Frank Lampard Senior of West Ham United went to watch a few Billericay games and saw enough to make a move.

The timing was fortunate; Steve had just been made redundant from the soap factory. But also, Billericay needed a new car park (Steve's fee was rumoured to have been spent on the tarmac for the job). When boyhood West Ham fan Steve Jones joined the club he'd always supported, the rarely trodden path from ordinary job to football hero was rendered as complete as the freshly laid asphalt in East Essex.

This kind of thing happened all the time in the '90s. John 'The Flying Postman' Williams – winner of a footrace among the fastest top-flight players at the 1992 Rumbelows Cup final – earned his nickname not on account of his ability to 'always deliver' from out wide (as I had been led to believe), but in fact because he used to be an actual postman.

Stuart Pearce only reluctantly packed in his electrician's business several years into his stint IN THE TOP FLIGHT, for Nottingham Forest. Of course, a player as honest as 'Psycho' refused to surreptitiously moonlight at first; he asked manager Brian Clough permission to carry on with his electrical trade in the evenings. Brian replied, "Yes, as long as you mend my kettle."

Pearce came to Quickly Kevin Towers to relay that anecdote, recalling his exasperated plea that, "The new element would cost more than the kettle," leading to a stand-off only settled by 'Psycho' buying Cloughie a new element out of his own pocket.

Another footballer with a job, who holds an unreasonably huge hold over my memory, was the pathetically named (prepare yourself) DJ Mellow D, aka Mr Danny Dichio.

It's hard to find evidence of exactly what records Danny (I refuse to use his DJ

> **The timing was fortunate; Steve had just been made redundant from the soap factory.**

name again) spun, outside of an interview in which he claims to like "early '90s rave stuff." More intriguing comments come from a 1996 interview with his QPR team-mate Trevor Sinclair who insists that while he amateurishly hacks at his decks at home playing "mainly US garage stuff," Danny proves himself "a class DJ." But what's more for Danny, Sinclair goes on to astonishingly claim that "being a footballer holds him back" from a more massive DJ career; which, for the first time ever, makes me grateful that his otherwise anonymous spell for the Superhoops at least prevented that awful DJ name-pun from reaching a wider audience.

But when it comes to jobs, you'd be hard

pressed to find someone with a more glittering LinkedIn profile than the man who helped wreck the English Italia 90 dream; mullet-topped, Geordie swooner Chris Waddle. Yet long before 'The Waddler' lit up the pop charts on account of his epic musical partnership with Glenn Hoddle performing 'Diamond Lights', Chris was lighting up the conveyor belt in a pork seasoning factory. NOT, as Chris is keen to point out in interviews, a sausage factory.

You can feel the seething, boiling anger still there long after retirement: "I never made sausages, just the seasoning. The press said I worked in a sausage factory for the headline writers. So if I was playing badly I was having a 'Banger' or if I was playing well, I was 'Sizzling.'"

You've got to feel sorry for the lad. That kind of journalistic error, at your expense, must be the absolute wurst.

Then there's Guy Whittingham's army stint. Ian Wright's time as a plasterer. Peter Schmeichel's year as an old people's home cleaner. Plus quite a few players who found a new vocation after their football career ended; some even finding success that outstripped their playing days. A case in point is ex-Arsenal and Palace stopper Andy Linighan's plumbing business, which has seen him driving around in a van emblazoned with the words: 'Average Footballer, Excellent Plumber'.

When you think back to these players with 'normal' jobs before becoming footballers, you realise they're an entirely different breed.

Back to Steve Jones, the first thing I noticed about him upon joining the Hammers (aside from his magnificent pair of early '90s 'curtains') was the fact that 'The Billericay Bombshell' looked nothing like his grizzled professional football colleagues, who hadn't had the luxury of a

nine-to-five in their formative years. Steve looked like a perma-tanned Adonis next to the growling likes of Martin Allen and Julian Dicks; who, by comparison, both looked like they'd eaten Billericay's new car park for breakfast.

Years later, I stumbled upon Steve Jones' other passion of collecting and distributing signed celebrity memorabilia on Twitter. Fast-forward a few months, I'm strolling through London's West End one summer Saturday morning, when I bump into the Bombshell and say 'hello'. Without hesitation, Steve showed me a picture of what appeared to be Anne Diamond that he'd just had signed by rock icon Bono outside his hotel.

After a brief chat and the realisation that photos of Anne Diamond are easily confused with early '80s shots of Bono, Steve bid me good morning and headed off up Oxford Street and into the day ahead.

I stood for a moment and considered the further evidence that '90s footballers were just like us and continue to be just that; going about their lives now, as they did then.

Earning a pound note. Grafting. People: just like the rest of us. Trying to find their way in the world, just like Anne Diamond when she recorded *The Joshua Tree*.

With the exception of the English third tier and below, nothing in '90s football was more route one than nicknames; Gazza, Smudger, Jonesy, etc. So it's nice to sit back and appreciate a nickname that couldn't be more on the plane-nose if it tried: Dennis Bergkamp's moniker, 'The Non-Flying Dutchman'.

Somewhat irrational fears were a huge deal in the '90s. Let's not forget that the decade began with a raft of big and small screen horrors which did nothing for anyone's sanity; there was a two-part TV adaption of Stephen King's *IT* (which did nothing for clowns), followed by the cinematic blockbuster *Arachnophobia* (which did nothing for spiders) and then *Bram Stoker's Dracula* (which did nothing for blood-sucking, centuries-old, undead Transylvanian types). But there's one fear I've always considered reasonable, and that's aviophobia: the fear of flying. And there's one man who will forever be linked to that fear in the mind of my generation: BA Baracus off *The A-Team*.

The show would eventually face criticism for the fact that its episodic structure hardly ever ventured outside of a set, oft-repeated format. And while I'd hate to validate that criticism, seemingly every episode of *The A-Team* does feature a scene whereby our protagonists would negotiate BA's refusal to fly anywhere by

sneaking up behind him with a chloroform rag and dragging his lifeless body on to a plane – straight into a third act that would inevitably feature a massive shoot-out in which no one got shot.

But whereas the A-Team always succeeded in getting their star man aboard an aircraft for the good of the gang, another, North-London based A-Team spectacularly failed. Because, as any '90s football fan would tell you, the Dutch were known for three things at that time: having a spectacular hatred of the Germans, getting spanked at Euro 96 by England and having a star player in Dennis Bergkamp who did not fly. Anywhere. Ever.

To be fair, he did at least have his reasons. In 1989, Surinam Airways Flight 764 from Amsterdam to Surinam crashed and took the lives of 15 Dutch players on their way to a friendly, many of whom Dennis had known personally. If their clubs hadn't blocked their call-ups, then '90s legends Ruud Gullit, Frank Rijkaard, Bryan Roy and Regi Blinker would also have been on that ill-fated flight.

Five years later, at the USA World Cup of 1994, Dennis's Netherlands team were held up at the airport after a journalist joked about having a bomb in his bag; a joke which cost that journo a spell in the slammer. In his autobiography, Dennis also mentions flying a small plane over Mount Etna near Naples some time later, getting into an air pocket and free falling for a few hundred, terrifying feet.

According to Bergkamp, by his last season at Inter Milan in 1995 the team were flying to away games in "those nasty little planes that stay in the clouds and shake all the time." He hated it so much, he claims to have spent time during away games, looking up at the clouds and worrying about how the weather was changing. After a final plane trip coming

THE A-TEAM™
A HEAVY LOAD!
©1983 Stephen J. Cannell Productions. All Rights Reserved.

back from a game with Fiorentina (a trip Dennis describes as a 'boneshaker'), enough was declared enough and Dennis decided never, ever, to fly again.

When his contract was drawn up as his move to Arsenal loomed closer, Dennis demanded it in writing: he was never to be obliged to fly anywhere. He'd later speculate that his refusal to fly cost him around 10 per cent of the value of his contract, but that he couldn't have cared: the Dutchman was not for flying.

And so, if ever the Non-Flying Dutchman was faced with a must-win European away tie, Pat Rice would fire up his Vauxhall Astra several days before, fill a carrier bag with Doritos and Fruit Pastilles, pick Dennis up, zip through the Eurotunnel and off to the continent in an Odd-Couple, laugh-out-loud road movie that's fun for all the family. Although, I do sometimes wonder if the whole situation could've been remedied by Arsene Wenger simply watching a bit more *A-Team*.

I vividly remember the birthday that my dad suggested Subbuteo as a present. I had seen the TV adverts suggestive of an all-action, atmospheric table-top game that faithfully recreated the drama and excitement of the real thing. The drama built even further after having arrived at the local toy shop and seeing an entire section dedicated to the world of what was fast becoming the favourite game I had never played.

A Premier League edition base set was purchased, containing the green baize, two breakable goals with wafer-thin nets, two Mitre Subbuteo balls, two sets of Subbuteo players (I believe it was a generic-enough red team with another generic blue team), a referee, two linesmen, a set of corner flags, a massive scoreboard and the Premier League trophy. I added two West Ham teams, home and away (obviously), but we weren't done yet.

Having some birthday money left over, my dad then offered to raise the stakes even further: "Why not get some of this other Subbuteo stuff?" The other Subbuteo stuff in question clearly offered nothing to the actual gameplay, but was incredibly stimulating to the young, imaginative mind. There were heaps of accessories to augment your Subbuteo set, and every one of them magical in its own way.

There were camera gantries and advertising hoardings. Floodlights, grandstands and corner stands. Orange balls (in case it snowed indoors?!) and Adidas Tango balls. All kinds of trophies, from the FA Cup to the World Cup. Then there were dugouts, complete with managers and coaching staff, through to packs of stewards in case the plastic crowd got too rowdy.

I had enough cash left over for a mini FA Cup, a grandstand and a dugout. On getting home after my *Supermarket Sweep*-style blitz of the Subbuteo section, I then set about assembling my booty. And as with any major footballing construction project, I thought of the fans first and the idea that it might be prudent to install the

grandstand before the action began.

It was two tiers, one set back from the other. Peculiarly, the length was only about one third of the length of the pitch. Which meant that when you put it up on the touchline, it had the effect of relegating my theatre of dreams to a Lincoln City-esque non-league arena; less a footballing cathedral and more of a footballing parish. With the stand assembled, however, I looked to fill it with my footballing faithful; the fans. But as I dipped back into the box to retrieve them, my suspension of disbelief creaked under the weight of one more setback, as it became obvious they were all entirely unpainted and fleshy

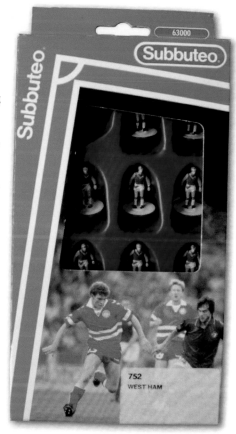

On getting home after my Supermarket Sweep-style blitz of the Subbuteo section, I then set about assembling my booty.

coloured; yes, my crowd was naked. Also, there clearly wasn't enough of them to fill the stand. Never mind, I thought, this looked great on TV so I must press on.

Half an hour later, having assembled a grandstand only 10 per cent filled – and filled with nudists, at that – I then took to sorting the pitch. The green baize had been compressed and folded in the box since it was first put there, so upon laying it on to the carpet of my bedroom it was a bumpy, uneven mess. This pitch was so bad it made Stamford Bridge's mid-'90s cabbage patch look like the green baize of a table at The Crucible. Even a quick go with the iron did nothing to sort it out.

And so, with a stadium full of undressed spectators and a pitch with more big lumps than Stoke City's starting line-up on a cold and wet Tuesday night, it finally came time to tackle the whole point of this ballyhoo and hoo-ha; actually playing a bloody game of Subbuteo.

My brother and I lined up our two teams, popped the ball in the middle of the pitch and prepared to clash for BOTH the FA Cup and Premier League trophies, in one match. But it's here that our problems really began, because I, like everyone else I've ever spoken to, never really fully understood the rules of Subbuteo.

Sure, we all read that little pamphlet thing that came with the box – but who really had the time to take it in, before laying out the players and cracking straight on with the chaotic and random flicking of players toward the ball?

I couldn't even tell you how long a game of Subbuteo was supposed to be. I had no idea if there's a half-time, no idea how often you can flick a player toward the ball,

what happened when the ball went out of play, or how to take goal-kicks. In fact, in researching this bit of the book just now, I've only just found out that you can only 'score' in Subbuteo from the final third of the pitch! Which makes a total mockery of pretty much every Subbuteo game I played, but also (sadly) every 70-yard Subbuteo screamer I've ever scored.

The game was incredibly difficult, bumpy

and my brother had soundly quit, it came time for my victorious boys to collect their grand prizes, both the FA Cup and Premier League trophies. However, for

> ## *Subbuteo games only ended when a player was stepped on and beheaded.*

my Subbuteo men, this posed quite a challenge, given that the Subbuteo-issued cups were about three times the size of the players. The player-to-prize ratio was all over the place. It was the real-life equivalent of Jordan Henderson winning the Premier League for Liverpool and then being expected to lift an 18-foot-high trophy over his head.

Today, I love whiling the hours away looking at Subbuteo accessories on eBay, or learning about the still-thriving, vibrant community of Subbuteo players, and especially seeing pictures of full stadiums.

The actual gameplay itself under-whelmed me; but that was never what Subbuteo was all about. The real glory lay in everything around it. The peripheral theatre, the accessories, the toy-shop excitement and, of course, the rows of naked Subbuteo fans on the terraces.

pitch or not. Plus, with the flimsy goalnets, moving your goalkeeper via the long green stick attached to his legs invariably destroyed any semblance of a properly positioned, FIFA-sanctioned goal frame. More often than not, the Subbuteo games I played only ended when one player had had enough, or accidentally stepped on and beheaded one of their players.

When all was said and done, however,

VIDEO GAMES

I n the '90s we didn't need sensational graphics, realistic gameplay or even real player names. Sensible Soccer gave us a top-down view, Pro Evo introduced us to Ronarid (ie Ronaldo) and Ruud vom Mistelroum (Ruud Van Nistelrooy), while FIFA let us outrun a yellow card. For many a '90s football fan, these games were just as iconic as the real matches, heroes and teams that defined our era. Let's meet a few of the classics.

Tecmo World Cup 90
For many fans of a certain generation, Italia 90 marked the start of their football fandom. It was a World Cup full of many iconic moments, and every fan who enjoyed that epoch-making tournament will have their own memories, no doubt burned into their retinas, forever.

However, when I think of Italia 90, my predominant memory – far more than the emergence of Cameroon or Gazza's tears – is becoming obsessed with Tecmo World Cup 90 whilst on a holiday to Spain. This was the first video game that bore any resemblance whatsoever to an actual game of football.

Sure, when passing to a team-mate, the ball would loop comically high in the air before arriving at their feet, no matter the distance. Sure, the game would DEFINITELY CHEAT, conspiring to ensure you didn't win the World Cup, meaning more coins would need to be added. And sure, the simulated crowd noise that would greet a goal was indistinguishable from TV static. But you never forget your first love: a pitch laid out horizontally, the ability to go on mazy runs, the chance to score a goal and have your team-mates run around like headless celebrating chickens. To go from nothing, to this, was to be living in the future; and it was glorious.

In hindsight, a few things were overlooked, such as the lack of player names. Also, there wasn't any semblance of formation; players just seemed to float around wherever they wanted. And not in a Dutch 'Total Football' way, I mean literally sometimes you wouldn't have a defence; they may have just wandered off for a fag break.

Yet watching old clips of it now on YouTube, being reminded of this gameplay of yesteryear, you can almost feel that arcade joystick in your hand. Tecmo World Cup 90 definitely still stands up.

> **There wasn't any semblance of formation; players just seemed to float around wherever they wanted.**

FIFA International Soccer (1993)
Tecmo World Cup was fantastic but the infrastructure needed to be able to play it at home (ie an arcade) was beyond everyone but the protagonist in 1994's *Richie Rich*. If you wanted to play a football video game at home, and you wanted a camera viewpoint that eschewed the less realistic top-down view of the game, then FIFA International Soccer – the first FIFA game in the now billion-dollar franchise – was here to rock your world.

Again, it was another game that completely reset what a football video game could be. And the sounds! From the opening sting – "E... A... Sports... It's in the game!" – right through to the sound that would accompany players kicking the ball (the noise was a bit like a balloon being kicked), and not forgetting the crowd reacting to everything on the pitch, the game was an immediate hit.

But let's get to the whole point of this

particular article and not beat around the bush. FIFA International Soccer had its flaws. And to this day I will maintain they are the greatest bugs in the history of video-game soccer.

Firstly, there was quite an easy way to score. All you had to do was send your striker to meander in front of the opposition keeper after he'd collected an errant ball; the absolute buffoon would then attempt to hoof the ball but only get as far as your face, allowing you to collect the football and ping it in from about two yards away. This glitch was no doubt the cause of many a family argument up and down the country, and often required a gentleman's agreement not to deploy it, lest a friendly game of FIFA could descend into violence off the pitch.

Secondly, and probably most famously of all, on FIFA 93, you had the option to foul an opponent. However, having committed a footballing offence, you could escape the wrath of the match official and the punishment you were due by an idea so genius I'm surprised modern footballers don't try it: running away from the ref. Yes, that's right. Having pushed or tackled an opponent into a heap, you could simply outrun your judgement day until the referee had had enough of chasing you and simply decided to play on, ignoring your indiscretion rather than carrying on the farcical chase all over the pitch.

The story goes that EA Sports did some research and figured out that a football video game was their best bet to break the European market. Their aim was 300k copies sold across the continent, over the release; but within the initial four weeks of sale they had sold 500k. Despite only coming out in December 1993, it finished up as the year's best-selling game.

It established the footballing video game like never before. It was great. It had an isometric camera angle. But best of all, let's be honest, you could outrun the ref.

International Superstar Soccer Pro
There are very few moments in a young boy's life that snap you into a new view of the world; moments that reveal something to you about existence that you had hitherto never even contemplated. For nearly all of my journey through school, my group of pals had largely aligned on everything apart from the football teams we chose to support; we had similar belief systems, hated the same teachers and embraced the same love of video games. The moment that rocked my world came in the summer of 1997,

when I went to my friend Dom's house and discovered that he, shock-horror, wasn't into FIFA and instead had got on board with a game that even to this day feels alien to me: International Superstar Soccer Pro.

The badges were there, the kits were there – but who the hell were these chaps playing for Italy? DeSinone? Galfano?! ALFREDO!? I'd watched enough *Gazzetta*

Football Italia to know they were all made up. And so, with no licences to speak of, I was ready to hate this game. But then I played it; and the silky way you could pass the ball around and control the players was undeniable. This was a good football game and my friend Dom possibly wasn't a total psychopath, after all (well, at least I did think that until he lost a game to my other mate and smashed his controller up against the wall, leaving us in his bedroom at his parents' house as he went AWOL).

FIFA 98: Road to the World Cup
There should be knighthoods dished out to the people involved in this game; for me, it is simply the greatest football video game in the history of the genre. As a

FIFA boy through and through, this game laid the foundations for every FIFA game to come with its attention to detail, the fact it had every team who COULD have qualified for the World Cup in '98, as well as the fact that it eschewed the previous isometric camera view for a proper TV-style presentation of the game. Then you chuck on top the fact it had a '90s commentary dream team of Andy Gray and John Motson on board, AND Des

Lynam in an effective anchor role.

We all have defining childhood Christmas memories, but few for me surpass the sheer wonder this game provided me as I went about attempting to secure World Cup qualification for Wales (no idea) on Christmas morning of 1997. Which lasted approximately four games, until my brothers and I decided that this was too hard and Wales were too shit.

It's also the first video game I can recall that had a memorable soundtrack, outside of the glorious but homespun audio provided by Sensible Soccer. FIFA 98 had Blur's 'Song 2' on it. That's like someone in the '60s saying, "Sure, the Beatles are great, but why don't we throw Mick Jagger and Keith Richards into the group as well?" That combination of great song and groundbreaking video game was shocking in its brilliance, it was almost too much.

But possibly the greatest aspect was its central theme: get a team to qualify for the World Cup. I don't ever recall there being an actual World Cup tournament after qualification, but there was something so niche and exciting about the idea of taking a nation and battling your neighbours in a bid to compete on the ultimate stage. It surprises me no football game has really focussed on such an adventure since, and it would be another 12 years before another FIFA game featured every FIFA nation in the world. Which, again, marks this out as a truly trailblazing title; I mean, who wouldn't jump at the chance to make Eritrea's World Cup dreams come true?!

Michael Owen's World League Soccer 99
Just as my grandad had settled on Betamax two generations before me, I plumped for Sega's Dreamcast when the next generation of consoles came out at the end of the decade, and thus continued a

long family tradition of backing soon-to-be-utterly-obsolete technology. However, for one brief shining moment, at roughly the same time as Sega took over JVC as Arsenal's sponsor, the Dreamcast looked like the platform of the future and had the footballing video game to prove it: Michael Owen's World League Soccer 99.

Of all the games on this list, it is easily the most underrated and easily the least discussed; it doesn't even have a Wikipedia page. But what it did have was incredibly flowing gameplay, *Football Italia*'s Pete Brackley and the irresistible ability to score 70-yard screamers.

For reasons known only to the game's developers and possibly Michael Owen, a decision had been made somewhere along the line to make insane long-range strikes on goal easier than scoring from inside the six-yard box. Players were also afforded the luxury of telekinesis; after you'd smacked the ball, you could curl

and twist the ball in flight as it made its way toward goal. Which often resulted in Cristiano Ronaldo-meets-Tony Yeboah Goal of the Season contenders... which in turn frequently made me ponder how Peter Brackley didn't pass out at the mere sight of them.

To be fair, it felt that Brackley had other problems if his commentary were to be taken at face value. Sometimes you don't know how good something is until you see something far inferior; which was the case as I went from Motson's eloquent patter on FIFA 98 to this title. Motson's intonation would flow effortlessly on FIFA, while Brackley on WLS 99 would sometimes sound like he was combining commentary with sticking a fork in a live plug socket.

He would quietly whisper "that's a lovely ball from" before bellowing "ADAMS!!!" Nothing compared to his fine work on *Football Italia*, but a wonderful game regardless.

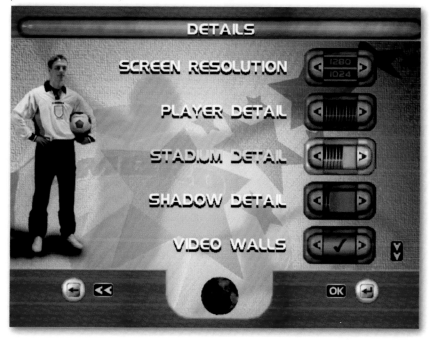

When you think of the great goals that defined the '90s, it's likely your mind's eye will conjure up images of Roger Milla at Italia 90, Matt Le Tissier down The Dell and David Beckham in South London. And sure, those goals were okay. But I'll tell you an even more impressive goalscoring feat: doing it at the wrong end in spectacular fashion, as your bemused team-mates and furious supporters look on.

No '90s Christmas was complete without a Danny Baker- or Nick Hancock-hosted VHS on the worst own goals of recent times. And so this book could hardly be called complete without committing the very best (and therefore the worst) '90s own goals to parchment...

Iain Dowie, West Ham v Stockport 1996
It was a cold, wet and blowy night in Greater Manchester as the Premier League's mighty West Ham United faced off with minnows Stockport County in the League Cup. With West Ham 1-0 up and cruising, Stockport found themselves with a throw-in by the corner flag. The ball is chucked in, headed out, then headed back in. Our hero, Iain Dowie, finds himself in acres of space defending his team's goal, and he rises like a salmon... provided that salmon's head had taken a pounding on the riverbed and lost all spatial awareness.

What happened next will forever have a place in football folklore.

Dowie absolutely buries that hopeful Stockport ball into the very corner of his own goal. The thousands of West Ham fans behind the goal watch on agog. The pace that famous head got on the ball gave the West Ham goalkeeper Ludek Miklosko not a chance in hell. The video of that own goal has hundreds of thousands of hits on YouTube, and should you ever attempt to search 'Iain Dowie', there's a good chance Google will auto-suggest the suffix 'Stockport own goal'; such was the career-defining nature of that incredible leap and baffling bullet header that preceded another scalp on Stockport's journey to the 1996 League Cup semi-final.

Lee Dixon, Arsenal v Coventry 1991
The first time I saw this goal was on Danny Baker's seminal, classic VHS *Own Goals and Gaffs* and, in the pre-internet age, it was the goal that had me most baffled. It went down in history as one of the quickest own goals of all time; but what the hell was wrong with Lee Dixon? Had he lost a bet? Surely, it was simply too good a goal to be a real own goal? Had Danny Baker made some sort of mistake with the inclusion of this footage?! It was unlike anything we'd seen before or since.

In the opening seconds of Arsenal's September 1991 League fixture against Coventry, Lee Dixon traps a ball in the full-back position, looks up at David Seaman, and deploys an ever-so-effortless chip over his head and into the goal. It defied all logic. Seaman had no chance, and Dixon just plonked his hands on his hips as the rest of Highbury looked on, slightly more silent than usual.

I suppose one excuse you could make on Lee's behalf was that this horrifying own goal occurred in the year before

the backpass rule was introduced, but even that doesn't forgive the absolute shellacking Lee gave the ball on its disastrous journey over Big Dave's head and into the annals of own-goal history.

John Pemberton, PSV v Leeds 1995
31st October 1995, and the Whites find themselves in Eindhoven in the UEFA Cup second round, taking on a highly stellar PSV (original Ronaldo played in this game) managed by the most Dutch man ever: Dick Advocaat. Leeds had scored three times in the first leg and yet still conspired to take a pasting, conceding five.

So the stakes were high in this second leg, that was until Phillip Cocu popped up 13 minutes into the game to put PSV into a pretty much unassailable position. As half-time approached, John Pemberton – perhaps driven to insanity by facing a young Brazillian on the verge of global stardom – reacted to a bobbling ball on the edge of the area by cutting it back into his own box with his right foot, then smashing it into the roof of his own net with his left.

John Lukic flung out a hand in a desperate attempt to preserve his team-mate's dignity, but it was no good. Pemberton clasps his head with his hands. PSV fans in the background celebrate and laugh (but mainly laugh). Ronaldo in the foreground has the temerity to awkwardly celebrate. Leeds went on to lose 3-0 on the night, 8-3 on aggregate.

Pemberton and Ronaldo; one went on to rightly be celebrated in this hallowed

 Lukic flung out a hand in a desperate attempt to preserve his team-mate's dignity.

document of all that was wonderful about '90s football, the other left for Barcelona later that summer.

Jamie Pollock, Man City v QPR 1998
No game on this list comes close to the tension that enveloped Maine Road at the tail end of the 1997/98 season, as Joe Royle's month-long reign faced its sternest test yet. It was a game that would prove pivotal in the years that followed. City, on the verge of dropping to the third tier of English football for the first time in their history, took on fellow relegation rivals QPR in a winner-takes-all clash, in the penultimate game of the season.

Anything other than a win would take City's fate out of their hands. This wasn't a time for fannying about. The professional footballers of Manchester City needed to go out and put on a footballing clinic in

brilliance, organisation and, above all else, calmness. Nothing else would do. Enter Jamie Pollock.

Jamie Pollock is a player best known to me, post '90s, for appearing on the same lists as the likes of Titi Camera, Neil Ruddock and Neil Shipperley – a group notable for how unrecognisable they've become, weight-wise, since their '90s pomp. But back in 1998, Jamie Pollock was a rarity in English football, his two games for Osasuna in 1996 marking him out as one of the few British players to have ventured into Spain before David Beckham had made it trendy. Mainly, however,

 What happened next lives somewhere between fame and infamy.

Pollock was known as a hard-working, tough-tackling midfielder; as evidenced by his spells at hard-working Middlesbrough and tough-tackling Bolton.

So with this supremely tense game in the balance at 1-1, no one could've predicted how Pollock would deal with QPR defender David Bardsley's nothing ball into City's defensive third. What happened next lives somewhere between fame and infamy; and nowhere is the dichotomy more present than in the title of the YouTube video for the goal: *Best/Worst Own Goal of All Time.* A video that has gained some 3.3 million views, by the way.

But back to Pollock. He races toward his own defence to deal with Bardsley's loose pass on the half volley. And objectively, everything about this darting run makes it look like Pollock is attacking the goal he's running to; QPR's striker even seems to start acting like a defender. Pollock latches on to the ball and, in a manner that is almost an exact carbon copy of Gazza's goal against Scotland at Euro 96, loops it over the QPR strikeforce and his own defender while accelerating to meet the ball as it falls; it genuinely is an astonishing piece of skill. But what happens next is arguably yet more adept. Pollock then meets the ball with his head and effortlessly loops it over goalkeeper Martyn Margetson's head; QPR lead 2-1.

But what's most hilarious about this incident is the reaction of the QPR players. Usually when an own goal is scored, there's at least one attacking player that a joyful team can focus their celebrations on; someone who put in a dangerous cross, someone who forced an error. But on account of Pollock's virtuoso own goal, there is literally no one on that QPR side to draw acclaim from anyone else. As a result, the players cheer individually, look at each other awkwardly and just trot back to their own half.

The game finished 2-2, but the damage was done. City won their last game away at Stoke but it only condemned both sides to relegation. But better news was to come for Jamie Pollock at the turn of the millennium as he beat off Jesus Christ to be voted the Most Influential Man of the Past 2000 Years in a poll that was later found to have been hijacked by a few thousand eternally grateful Rangers fans.

THE UK's BEST SELLING GOALKEEPER GLOVES

Bring it in. Who wouldn't want a bear hug off of Big Nev?

Growing up in the '90s, the festive period was classically a time of merriment, VHSs and replica football shirts; but also, crucially, a time when new football boots were received.

Football boots have always been something of a curiosity. This is probably because your average '90s football fan experienced their peak footballing nerdiness at the same time as the advent of exotic neon football footwear bursting on to the scene in contrast to the standard black boots of the previous 100-odd years.

Until the dawn of the Premier League, football boots were never much of 'a thing'.

You pretty much had either the Adidas Copa Mundial or the Puma King... but that was literally it. They were the only boots anyone had, and everybody accepted the fact. There was a certain peace that came with not having much of a choice to make.

But all that changed in 1994 when Craig Johnston invented an entirely new boot: the Predator.

Older readers may remember Craig Johnston for blazing a trail for Australian footballers in England, long before the

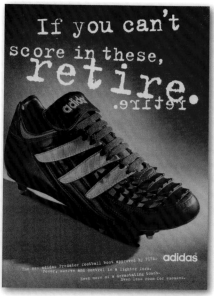

If you can't score in these, retire.

The new adidas Predator football boot approved by FIFA. adidas
Power, swerve and control in a lighter form.
Even more of a devastating touch.
Even less room for excuses.

documentary about the design of the new Predator boot and the science behind its making. In this film, Craig explained that the new boot would feature a special rubber material along the upper striking area of the boot in order to enhance the thrust and spin of the ball.

He then explained that the rubber in

> **The rubber in question was the same used in those ridiculously bouncy balls.**

question was the same rubber used in those ridiculously bouncy balls that were also a sensation in the '90s. You couldn't fault the logic.

Hearing this, it immediately struck me that these new football boots were the closest thing football boot manufacturing would ever come to 'magic boots'. I had visions of suddenly becoming much more than a bang-average, lanky striker

likes of Robbie Slater and Stan Lazaridis. It was presumably for this honour that Johnston earned the route-one, unimaginative nickname of 'Skippy'.

As I recall, Craig Johnston starred in a

(perhaps, dare I dream, even a slightly above-average one).

Instantly, the boots were on my Christmas list. But my next concern was; when would the entire West Ham and England team get decked out in them? They were, after all, essentially magic football boots! If we stole a march on the rest of the clubs, we'd have the Premier League sewn up by the New Year!

I recall several weeks passing before I saw one Hammer emerge from the Upton Park tunnel decked out in Adidas

Predators. I couldn't believe my eyes. Of all the players best suited to the ergonomic rubber technology of the boot, you'd struggle to find a more questionable candidate than... Mr Iain Dowie.

As I'm sure Iain himself would admit, he wasn't best known for his swerving shot,

fancy footwork or slick passing.

In fact, it's fair to say he was known for absolutely none of those things (although it's a little-known fact that Dowie has a Master's Degree in Engineering).

Also, it's probably an understatement to say that Dowie's game was approximately 90 per cent centred around his infamous

 I'm sure Iain himself would admit he wasn't best known for his swerving shot.

head. So why on earth had this magic boot ended up on his feet before anyone else's?!

Needless to say, the impact the famous Predator boot had on our protagonist was negligible, although it did give Iain a mighty lift as he soared above everybody to score that own goal away to Stockport in the League Cup in 1996.

So, to conclude, while the Adidas Predator went on to become synonymous with Steven Gerrard, David Beckham and Zinedine Zidane, it did not become synonymous with Iain Dowie, or indeed, with me. And, thus, the hunt for a magical football boot goes on; actually, did I mention Iain Dowie is a *bona fide* rocket scientist? Surely, he is more qualified than Johnston to invent the magic boot! What's he waiting for?

Nineties football was packed full of characters you could quite easily categorise, some we even deal within this book, eg the fat player, the player with a real job on the side and managers with flat caps. But there's one category of player that sadly went extinct around the same time Keane and Vieira scrapped in the Highbury tunnel: the hard men. Here's a few unhinged nutters that I sincerely hope never read this chapter.

Vinnie Jones

Long before Vincent Peter Jones burst on to the acting scene with his portrayal of characters known for their menacing brutality, Hertfordshire's most famous footballing Welshman was marauding football grounds, striking fear, and studs, into the hearts of opposing teams around the country. And like any good '90s football hard man, he combined the two traditions of coming up through the non-league ranks while maintaining the sideline profession of hod carrier.

He signed for Wimbledon from Wealdstone for the modest fee of £10,000 and, two years later, had won the FA Cup against Liverpool in one of the all-time great cup upsets – this despite nearly turning Steve McMahon's legs to dust with an opening-minutes tackle that bordered on grievous bodily harm. A year before that triumph, Vinnie also created a legendary pop-culture moment when an eagle-eyed photographer snapped him attempting to crush a young Gazza's testicles, with his bare hands, during a League game for the Dons against Newcastle.

In addition to 12 career red cards, Vinnie also has the honour of holding the record for the quickest-ever booking; yes, three seconds is plenty long enough for our legendary '90s hard man to leave his mark on Sheffield United's Dane Whitehouse. As Vinnie himself would say in his autobiography of that incident: "I must have been too high, too wild, too strong or too early, because, after three seconds, I could hardly have been too bloody late!"

Graeme Souness

The captain of Liverpool's incredibly successful '80s team, Graeme Souness is your archetypal footballing hard man slash nutter. With a moustache that seemed to lay the foundations for fictional Scottish loose cannon Begbie in *Trainspotting*, Souness was every bit the intimidating and terrifying presence of his era. Yet somehow, as his playing days came to an end, he contrived to find a way to become even more frightening from the touchline. When Kenny Dalglish handed in his notice in February 1991, in came our Graeme with a footballing philosophy that seemed almost exclusively about building the most brutal football squad this side of 'Chopper' Harris. Efforts were made to dispense with the likes of the respectable old guard, Ian Rush and John Barnes, and in came a new breed of rash and unpredictable characters in Julian 'The Terminator' Dicks,

Neil 'Razor' Ruddock and David 'The Vampire' James (the latter so-called as he was 'scared of crosses').

The experiment failed in January 1994. Souness was jobless. But in a match made in hell, Galatasaray welcomed a Scotsman who would go on to become a legend in Istanbul after one single season in charge.

Souness seemed to find a way to become even more frightening from the touchline.

As the 1995/96 season came to its climax, Souness had successfully steered Galatasaray to the Turkish Cup final, up against bitter enemies Fenerbache at their Sukru Saracoglu Stadium, in a fixture nicknamed 'The Eternal Rivalry'.

Having led Gala to a famous victory and the Turkish Cup, some bright spark handed Souness a Galatasaray flag which Graeme then saw fit to plant bang in the centre-circle of their most notorious, hated and uneasy-going rivals; the result, obviously, was a riot.

As the realisation dawned on Souness that he may have sparked World War III, he legged it toward the dressing room, but not without incident. As he later explained in 2018: *"Just as I got into the tunnel I got a thump on the side of the head. A supporter had gotten into the tunnel. So I had a bit of a tussle with him and eventually got back to the safety of the dressing rooms."*

Having safely dispatched a fan via the medium of a fist fight, Graeme then prepared himself for the inevitable pasting his bosses would inflict upon him: *"Once I got into the dressing room, I thought, 'Once the directors come down, that's it. I'm going to be sacked on the spot and on the first plane out of here tomorrow...*

"But it was the exact opposite. Some of them had tears in their eyes, and I've never been hugged and kissed by so many men in such a short period of time.

"They were absolutely delighted, obviously, that we'd won the Cup, but they seemed even more delighted that I'd planted the flag in the Fenerbahce stadium."

To this day, Gala fans hold Souness in such high esteem that he holds the nickname 'Ulubatli Souness', after supporters likened his actions to those of legendary Ottoman warrior Ulubatli Hassan who himself had planted a flag in victory at a far less intense conflict known as the 'Siege of Constantinople' in 1453. And more recently, in 2014, Gala fans once more celebrated this incident by unfurling a 100ft mural in honour of Souness just before another instalment of The Eternal Derby against Fenerbahce.

Stuart Pearce

To say the next man on our list is hard as nails would imply that nails have anything like the pain threshold of Shepherds Bush and England's favourite Psycho, Stuart Pearce.

As an aspiring young footballer his dad once gave him a single piece of advice, which he pretty much built an entire career on: "Never let them know you're hurt."

But before we get into Stuart's ability to take an incredible amount of pain, we should perhaps first mention his ability to inflict it.

The story goes that the then Coventry manager, Bobby Gould, had been tipped off about a non-league left-back/electrician currently plying his trade at Wealdstone. Sure enough, Bobby picked up the tip and drove to see the proto-Pearce in action; within minutes of the kick-off, Psycho had clattered an opposing player into the stand. Bobby bid for him that night, and Pearce thus jumped from non-league to the top footballing division in the country.

Stuart became one of the nation's most elite left-backs as a result of his ability, the pride he took in his performances, but more than anything, the fact he was so obviously fearless. Psycho first came to national, celebrity-level prominence when his penalty was saved at the semi-final of Italia 90, contributing to England's defeat to West Germany on penalties. The tears after, alongside Gazza's, marked Psycho out as an unforgiving hard man with a heart.

Fast-forward two years to Euro 92 and the one highlight England fans can extract from that forgotten tournament is the way Pearce reacts to a headbutt from Basil Boli. With Psycho's attention drawn elsewhere, Boli runs up and headbutts Pearce on the chin; the victim falls to the floor, but almost immediately jumps back up and returns to his position, blood streaming from his chin. A reaction absolutely consigned to the '90s.

Pearce later revealed that he knew full well that Boli was responsible. But rather than blame Boli, he pinned accountability on the player he was marking for the rest of the game; thus cleverly forcing two

> **Within minutes of the kick off, Psycho had clattered an opposing player into the stand.**

opposing players to spend the rest of the game in fear of retribution.

A further statement of his hard-man credentials came at the end of the decade for West Ham. Sustaining an injury in the first half of a match against Watford, Pearce played on for a few minutes until half-time; the injury, it was discovered during the break... was a broken leg. Even when informed of this, Psycho attempted to argue he could run it off.

Stuart Pearce was one of the most frightening personalities of '90s football. He set the example for all '90s hard men that followed, including a new, young Irish signing who joined Nottingham Forest from Cobh Ramblers in 1990. A young man who would later say: "When I was at Forest, Stuart Pearce was captain, and he was intimidating in that he pushed people, but I wasn't scared – I loved it. I looked at Stuart Pearce, like, 'Right, that's what you have to do to become a great player...'"

Roy Keane

There is so much to admire about Roy Keane. His tenacious tackling. His forthright leadership. His incessant dog-walking. But for me, outside of his generally terrifying demeanor, the characteristic I most associate with Roy Keane is his ability to hold a long-standing grudge for an inordinate amount of time.

Keane's hard-man credentials are best represented in the retelling of his infamous rivalry (if you can call it that) with Norwegian defender, and Erling Haaland's dad, Alf-Inge. It starts in September 1997 at Elland Road. United in their late '90s pomp, chasing a title. Leeds falling from their early '90s heyday, not yet at their 2001 Champions' League zenith, but substantially better off than the financial implosion that followed that particular folly.

Leeds go 1-0 up through unrenowned goalscorer David Wetherall on 34 minutes; after that point the game is bogged down by a combination of bitty challenges, a Leeds defence that frustrates the United forward line and the efforts of a certain Leeds Norwegian frustrating a certain United Irishman. Even the introduction of Ben Thornley could do nothing to salvage a point for Sir Alex's men.

Roy's second autobiography, *The Second Half,* revealed the frustration of playing against the original (and best) Haaland in 2014: *"He was an absolute prick to play against. Niggling, sneaky."*

With the clock ticking down, the newly introduced Ben Thornley slid through what was to become a literal hospital pass for Roy Keane; he chased it down and as Haaland closed in, Roy swung a leg across Alf-Inge to take him out, but in doing so, took himself out for a year with a torn cruciate ligament.

What came next sealed Haaland's fate. With Keano prostrate on the Elland Road turf, rolling in agony, Alf-Inge stepped in to give him a volley of verbals that would have made John McEnroe blush. Roy Keane missed most of the 1997/98 season; Arsenal won the League that year after United blew an eleven-point lead.

Fast-forward four, YES FOUR LONG YEARS, and it's April 2001. United v City, the Manchester derby. With the score tied 1-1 and five minutes left on the clock, Keane and Haaland get the opportunity to lock horns in the middle of the field; but rather than engage in a competitive tussle for the football, Keano decides to try and snap Haaland's leg in half and settle a score from four years previous.

As Keane would later write in his autobiography: *"I'd waited long enough. I f**king hit him hard. The ball was there (I think). Take that you c**t. And don't ever stand over me sneering about fake injuries".* But then again, he also said in an interview regarding the incident that he had made *"a genuine effort to play the ball";* which is just about as absurd as his four-year grudge or indeed Sir Alex Ferguson's claim that he didn't see the tackle that resulted in Roy's most notorious career red card.

When Paul Gascoigne returned from Italia 90 he was a man in demand. After the tears in Turin, the whole country had taken the cheeky chappie into their hearts. His story was real *Roy of the Rovers* stuff. Who amongst us hadn't dreamt of playing for our boyhood football club, representing our country at the World Cup, then one day sporting a pair of enormous comedy boobs on an open-top bus parade through our nation's capital?

Gazzamania, as the papers dubbed it, was officially sweeping the country. Which meant a tidal wave of media opportunities for the Geordie genius. One minute he was chatting happily to good old Terry on *Wogan*, the next he was centre stage with Lindisfarne on *Top of the Pops*.

Wherever he went he was headline news, always surrounded by cameras and always wearing a horrible signature shell suit, just for good measure.

With their client's profile reaching fever pitch, Gascoigne's agents wasted no time in cashing in. You could slap the Gazza brand on any old toot and it guaranteed

sales. Which explains the alliance with MB (makers of the iconic Connect 4) to rebrand ailing board game Kick-off! into Gazza! The Game.

Kick Off! was a simplistic two-player game with a cardboard football pitch divided into a grid. The players would then use cards, which had numbers and directions on them, to determine how many grid spaces forward/left/right they could progress before having a shot at goal. Much like association football, it was

> ## With their client's profile reaching fever pitch, Gascoigne's agents wasted no time in cashing in.

a test of strategy and sometimes pure luck. Despite the rebrand, the gameplay stayed the same as it had for years. Which meant that whilst Gazza was proudly plastered over the box, the grainy sketches on the playing cards didn't feature our hero or

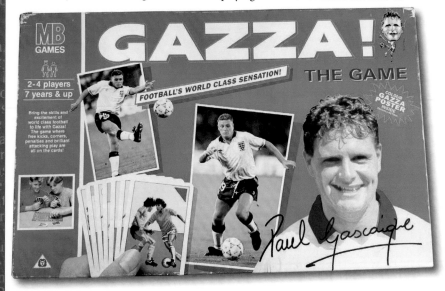

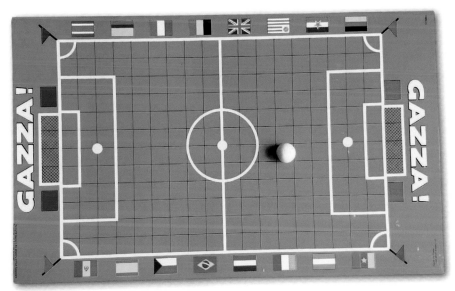

any of his contemporaries. They looked more like players from the 1940s who had just stepped off the beach at Normandy.

All in all, it was harmless fun. Yet ironically this was exactly the type of game you could imagine Gazza would absolutely loathe to its core.

Notorious for having an attention span shorter than a wasp in a room full of jam jars, you can't picture him lasting past two turns in the game before setting the board on fire, shoving it up Jimmy Five Bellies' bum crack, and betting his best pal 100 quid that he couldn't make it to the sink before the flames started scorching his ringpiece.

In the days before Jeff Stelling and blanket TV coverage, matchdays on the sofa were a celebration of '90s multimedia in all its glory. With no single information source, we were reliant on our eyes and ears to solve the mystery of how our team was faring on a Saturday afternoon. We all had our own rituals, a triumph of trial and error. Though most involved these key elements:

2.55pm: Telly on. Teletext on. Page 302 or 140, depending on which screen had fewer characters missing. Head to the page displaying the latest scores. Extra time allotted in case you wanted to squeeze in a quick game of Bamboozle to calm the pre-match nerves.

3pm: Radio on, tuned to 5 Live, with live match commentary (almost never the game you were most concerned about), but at least there was around-the-grounds coverage as soon as the goals went in... Just as long as those goals didn't happen to coincide with the racing from Chepstow. In which case, you're doomed to four more minutes of agony, wondering what you might have missed.

3.45pm: A welcome half-time reprieve from the frantic manoeuvring between different media. Head over to *Grandstand* as Steve Rider calmly directs traffic from reporters around the country, provided the bastard rugby league hasn't overrun.

4pm: Back to Teletext and radio for the second half. It was occasionally nerve-jangling stuff. A goal might appear on Teletext, but there would be no official word on the radio. Was it a goal? Was it a mistake? Seconds seemed like minutes, minutes seemed like hours. The joy of

celebrating a goal paralysed by fear of an administrative error. That's what it was like when you relied on such backward technology. Thankfully these days we've got VAR to do that for us.

4.39pm: An all-important double substitution as Teletext and radio are given a well-deserved breather while Rider and the Vidiprinter bring us the crescendo of the day's play – provided the bastard rugby league hasn't overrun again.

5pm: At last, time for the match reports. Waiting for Teletext's finest authors to sum up 90 minutes of sheer hell in 80 words or less. It's an extraordinary skill. The enemy of any writer is his word count, but doing justice to, for example, a six-goal thriller within that sort of storytelling limit is a near-impossible task. Equally, when some games are so horrifically f**king awful that task could seem as colossal as translating the Old Testament. Which brings me to my favourite match report of all time.

Imagine all that stress. All that angst. Imagine the horror of that anxious wait for any precious morsel of information about the match. And then you're greeted by this: "Bloke had a stinker; his team lost".

Simple game, football.

128

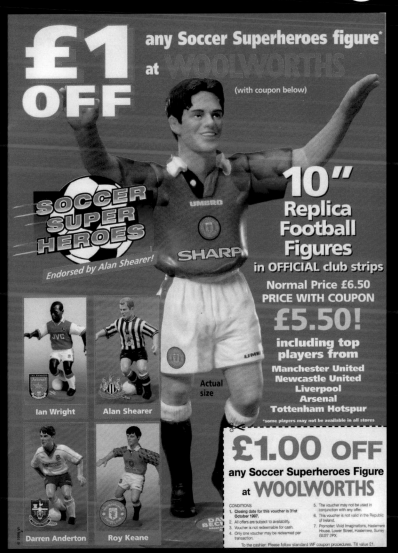

There's a vicious rumour that Juninho's replica was life-size.

El Tel. You remember him. Euro 96 and all that. The former England manager has been many things in life. On the pitch he created an iconic Crystal Palace side in the late '70s, became the head honcho at the Nou Camp in the '80s, and led his country to the brink of glory in the '90s.

Off the pitch his life was equally colourful, though somewhat less successful. The Chelsea tailors he opened with George Graham and 'Chopper' Harris in the '70s went bankrupt. And he was found guilty by the Department of Trade and Industry of "deception, bribery, lying and manipulation of accounts" whilst in charge of Tottenham Hotspur plc and three other companies he ran during the late '80s and early '90s. Just for good measure, whilst the DTI were reaching their verdict he was simultaneously taking Portsmouth (where he had a controlling interest) to the brink of bankruptcy in 1998. In for a penny, in for a pound, as they say. Unless, of course, you were one of his creditors.

But it was almost impossible to dislike the man. Maybe it was his cheeky cockney smile. Or his japes with Des and Jimmy in the *Match of the Day* studio. Or the fact that he refused to give Carlton Palmer another international cap. Whatever it was, Venables' ability to gleefully try his hand at anything in search of a few quid made him even more of a loveable rogue.

Which brings us on nicely to one of his lesser-known ventures: when he tried to crack the elusive board-game market. Back in 1990, Venables paired with publishing giant Waddingtons to bring the world of football management into our living rooms. And he was going to do it in his own inimitable style.

Never knowingly accused of lacking ambition, El Tel wanted to create a game that captured his unique experience of boot rooms and boardrooms in a format that promised fun for all the family. Hence, Venables didn't just invite you to play... he invited you to step right into his size nine Chelsea boots and *be* The Manager.

They call being the England boss 'the 'impossible job', and anyone who had the misfortune of playing this game would

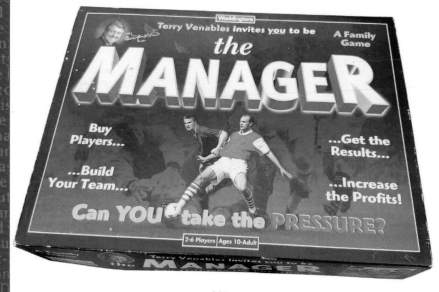

130

realise that Terry Venables was the perfect man for the national team hotseat. Because if you could be good at this game, then life should hold no fears for you ever again.

It was an extraordinary maelstrom of football, finance and, bizarrely, light entertainment. Let's start with the football. Your task was to build a successful team that met the expectations of both supporters and shareholders, because, as Venables himself said on the blurb: "Football is a game, but it's also a business. And at the end of the day, the one with the most money will win."

Of course to achieve this Valhalla of football finance, many of your decisions were based on the roll of a dice (the more

❝ It was an extraordinary maelstrom of football, finance and, bizarrely, light entertainment. ❞

cynical amongst you would suggest this perfectly mirrored some of Venables' accounting practices).

Roll the wrong number and you could find your star striker on his way to your nearest rivals, roll the right one and you could find yourself on the end of an unexpected windfall to keep the bank manager happy. Assuming the bank manager accepted the game's own form of currency, of course. Which he did, thankfully, because the bank manager was no less then El Tel himself.

The sensationally named 'Banco de Venables' handed out notes with the great man's face and name adorning all the denominations right up to £1 million. With the benefit of hindsight, you'd be forgiven for losing yourself in a rabbit hole of possibilities about this particular

financial institution. Maybe there's a parallel universe where the Banco de Venables has been at the heart of football's most baffling transactions:

"Hello, is that Banco de Venables? Look, we're redeveloping Wembley Stadium and ideally we'd like the project to overrun considerably, thereby incurring crippling interest payments, and come in roughly three times over budget. Any chance you could front us the money?"

"Dear Banco de Venables. We are writing to you today with the aim of securing £800,000 investment for a new striker. We've never seen him live and are relying purely on grainy VHS footage. But we believe Marco Boogers to be a sound investment for the club's future. Anyway, bung us a few quid would ya? Much obliged."

"To whom it may concern, further to my recent notice regarding the purchase of Seth Johnson from Derby County, I can confirm that agreement has now been reached with the club. He's on £5k a week at his current club, but with a bit of negotiating we reckon we can get him for £37k a week here. Please send us the wonga via our financial advisor in the Cayman Islands."

However, once you had successfully

negotiated the dice-fuelled minefield of your financial destiny, there was an element of skill to the game that ultimately determined your success.

And this was where the game's creators really attempted to capture the imagination of all the family. The football world wasn't nearly as diverse, as all-consuming as it is today, and fearing that wives and daughters might not be able to drag themselves away

from *EastEnders* on Christmas Day on the premise of football's profitability, the good folk at Waddingtons embarked on a bold strategy: give it a sprinkling of general knowledge and light entertainment.

The consequence was the most extraordinary set of question cards since records began.

And a series of far-flung answers that are unlikely to share the same physical space ever again...

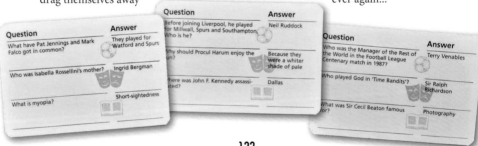

Question	Answer
What have Pat Jennings and Mark Falco got in common?	They played for Watford and Spurs
Who was Isabella Rossellini's mother?	Ingrid Bergman
What is myopia?	Short-sightedness

Question	Answer
Before joining Liverpool, he played for Millwall, Spurs and Southampton. Who is he?	Neil Ruddock
Why should Procul Harum enjoy the sun?	Because they were a whiter shade of pale
Where was John F. Kennedy assassinated?	Dallas

Question	Answer
Who was the Manager of the Rest of the World in the Football League Centenary match in 1987?	Terry Venables
Who played God in 'Time Bandits'?	Sir Ralph Richardson
What was Sir Cecil Beaton famous for?	Photography

AD NAUSEAM

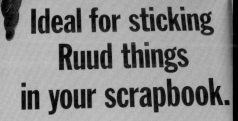

**Ideal for sticking
Ruud things
in your scrapbook.**

SPECIAL EDITION FOOTBALL STI(
FROM PRITT

Available in Arsenal, Aston Villa, Man Utd, Chelsea & Liverpool

You can imagine Ruud Gullit looking mournfully through his scrapbook of European Cup wins alongside Rijkaard and Van Basten, before going into training with new team-mates Erland Johnsen and Paul Furlong.

133

Jean-Claude Van Damme, Jackie Chan, Jet Li – there were some very dangerous feet kicking around throughout the '90s, though perhaps none with the ferocity of Stephen George Bull. Born and bred in the Black Country, Bull made his name at local club Tipton Rovers, balancing manual labour work with the hard graft of non-league football. The semi-professional game was made for a player like him: scrapping with centre-halves from first whistle to last, smashing in goals on pitches which made the Somme look like a snooker table, then downing pints of mild in the bar afterwards.

Bully's goal-a-game ratio earned him a move to West Bromwich Albion, but he was eventually considered too raw for the top tier of English football and was discarded from the Hawthorns for having a first touch like a harpoon.

So, he arrived at Wolverhampton Wanderers in 1986. Or at least the crumbling remains of the mighty Wolves. By this time Molineux was in such a state of disrepair, you wouldn't blame the groundsman for buying a time-share in Chernobyl. The players trained in the car park or local amenities strewn with dog shit, and crowds had dwindled down to a few thousand.

The days when 50,000+ would turn up to worship the great Billy Wright were a distant memory. This decaying monolith of a club needed a new hero. And in Steve Bull, affectionately nicknamed 'The Tipton Skin', they got one.

It's hard to accurately describe Bull's style of play. He had all the technical finesse of a Tyrannosaurus Rex chasing a steak and onion pasty. He was a raw talent who relished the physicality of the lower leagues. If the centre-half gave him a kick, Bull puffed his chest out, put his elbows up

and got ready to dish out a receipt. Soon defenders looked forward to facing Bull as much as Superman fancied a Kryptonite sandwich.

His goalscoring figures were positively heroic. Two 50-goal seasons in the late '80s as Wolves sealed successive promotions. For many of us, actual sightings of Bull in the wild were few and far between. However, his name became well known thanks to its regular appearances in the classified scores section of *Shoot!*, *Match* and the top scorers chart on Ceefax.

> " *This decaying monolith of a club needed a new hero. And in Steve Bull, 'The Tipton Skin', they found one.*

The zenith of his career was undoubtedly in 1988/89. Bully had just finished a season in the third tier, where his tally of 50 goals propelled Wolves to promotion. Despite the fact he'd never set foot in the Second Division, Bully was summoned for England international duty by Bobby Robson. He scored on his debut at Hampden Park, much to the delight of a raucous England following.

He started the new decade in spectacular fashion. He was shitfaced. Ahead of a New Year's Day fixture at Newcastle, Bully treated himself to a couple of pints the night before, then a couple more. By kick-off he smelled like he'd had a pre-match soak in a bath of Stella Artois. His first-half performance was a catastrophe. He was seeing three balls, and they were all bouncing off his shins, his knees and his arse at regular intervals. What happened in the second 45 minutes is the stuff of legend. Bull emerged like a man possessed and smashed all four goals in a 4-1 win for the visitors.

Later that season season he netted twice in a 4-2 win over Czechoslovakia at Wembley where only a magnificent Paul Gascoigne performance stole the headlines. When the beloved striker was called up by Bobby Robson for Italia 90, it was feted far beyond the Black Country. This was a man who'd never played regular top-flight football. He didn't drive a Jag. He didn't have a sponsorship deal. He had the showbiz factor of a packet of pork scratchings, and he didn't care a jot. He was everyman. The regular Joe who'd risen from the factory line to the Football League. And fans loved him for it.

Those who worried how a man of simple tastes might fare on foreign soil needn't have. The local newspapers back home encouraged fans to send well-wishes overseas and soon Bully was besieged with

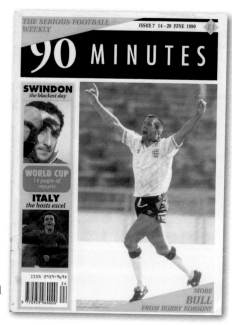

sacks of mail wishing him luck for his World Cup adventure. In the event, Bull made four appearances in Italy, including a start against Egypt. Bizarrely, they turned out to be his last caps. Incoming boss Graham Taylor, who preferred an agricultural style of football, decided Wolverhampton's finest lacked the finesse for world level.

So Bully was left to roam the pastures of England's second tier, which he did with his customary aplomb. In the space of a decade his prolific strike rate transformed Wolves from Fourth Division paupers to the brink of the top flight.

Sadly, they always seemed to fall at the final hurdle and one of English football's greatest goal machines never did set foot in the Premier League. There were no *Super Sundays* or *Monday Night Footballs* for Steve Bull. Just a lot of Saturday afternoons the length and breadth of the Football League banging in goal after goal and loving every second of it.

In 1873 famous French poet Arthur Rimbaud wrote his prose poem *Une Saison en Enfer (A Season in Hell* to you, guv), which became one of the most debated literary works of the era, influencing artists, writers, musicians and even filmmakers to this very day.

It centres on a man at war with himself. A man with dual identities. The first saw light and charm at every turn, cherishing the wonder of life. The second felt he was surrounded by idiots and loathed the hysteria of his chosen profession.

As Manchester United striker Eric Cantona sat before the baying press corps in 1995, having escaped a prison sentence by the skin of his teeth, perhaps he felt some kindred spirit with his countryman of yore.

for football's own *enfant terrible*. He'd maintained throughout that he'd been provoked by the Palace supporter's tirade of abuse – an accusation which the gentleman in question firmly denied. "Off you go, Cantona. It's an early bath for you," was his version of events, which sounds a bit like Brutus claiming he deposited the blade in Julius Caesar's back "because he

> *Now here he was, presumably ready to bestow the baying press corps with a lengthy mea culpa.*

Admittedly, Rimbaud had never won successive Premier League titles, stomped a mudhole in John Moncur's chest, or kung-fu kicked a Crystal Palace supporter on a stormy night at Selhurst Park. But let's not sweat the small stuff.

Flanked by the Manchester United hierarchy, Cantona was due to give a statement on his successful appeal against his legal punishment for going feet-first into the opposition fans on that fateful February night. An appeal which meant that rather than residing at Her Majesty's Pleasure, he would be returning to his Premier League home in the near future.

It was the finale to a tempestuous few months

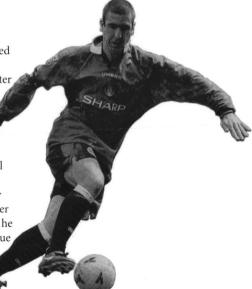

couldn't find any pockets."

And having been handed a hefty fine and lengthy ban by the Football Association, Cantona had been on the brink of retirement, only for a heartfelt letter from Alex Ferguson to coax him back into the fold. Now here he

> *Things got heated as the panel harked back to his conduct that infamous day at Norwood Junction.*

was, presumably ready to bestow the baying press corps with a lengthy *mea culpa*.

Except he wasn't. "When the seagulls follow the trawler, it is because they think sardines will be thrown into the sea," were the Frenchman's only remarks on the matter.

It left onlookers flabbergasted. Football had a chequered relationship with bird life at the best of times. "Sick as a parrot" was a common cliché in football management circles. Though Jack Charlton took it a step further when he said, "See ya, lads. I'm off grouse shooting," after his Newcastle side got pumped in midweek at Arsenal in 1984 (he didn't return until 1.45pm on Saturday afternoon, apparently).

It wasn't to be Cantona's last poetic outburst. In 2001, on the French debate show *Côté Tribune*, things got heated as the panel harked back to his conduct that infamous day at Norwood Junction. Cantona took issue with the journalists who labelled his behaviour as "unforgivable", claiming that if the Rolex-wearing Pope, as he described him, could forgive the countless atrocities of the Catholic Church during the Crusades, then surely his punch-up at Palace was worthy of absolution.

His final words? "I'd piss in the Pope's ass." Rimbaud couldn't possibly have put it any better.

I n the '90s there was nothing better than a World Cup summer. It offered a blessed relief from the traditional three-month abyss between the football season ending and starting up again, particularly for those who couldn't entertain another England batting collapse at the hands of Curtly Ambrose.

A World Cup summer was punctuated by several high points. There was the announcement of the respective pundit line-ups on BBC and ITV, which would trigger much musing as to how messrs Hill, Hansen and Ginola would gel in the pressure-cooker situation of a TV studio. Then there was the hotly anticipated release of the musical soundtracks. And finally, when the first-round proper was underway, we'd get our first glimpse of Des Lynam, looking splendid in his summer wardrobe, previewing the next 30 days of thrills and spills with the nonchalance of a man watering his geraniums.

At home, there were two essential accompaniments required by any self-respecting football fan. Firstly, as we discuss elsewhere in this book, there was the sticker album. No sooner had the final whistle blown on the domestic season than the bell rang to signal the opening of the sticker trading market. Frantic negotiations filled morning, noon, and night as we scrabbled to fill our squads ahead of the big kick-off.

Secondly, there was the World Cup wallchart, which offered an altogether more genteel experience. Unfolding a chart in all its glory was akin to surveying a lost medieval tapestry. Hours could be lost staring at its sacred text, searching for deeper meaning. How might England make it to the final? Where would Jurgen

> *Unfolding a wallchart in all its glory was akin to surveying a lost medieval tapestry.*

138

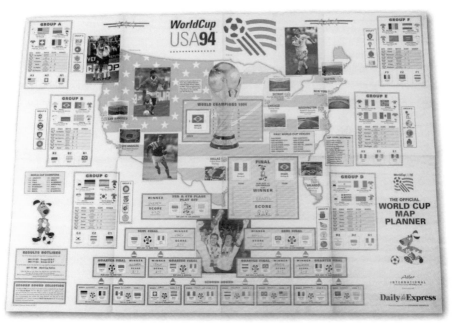

Klinsmann win his first hotly disputed penalty? And which hardworking Swedish midfielder would eventually pitch up at Sheffield Wednesday?

It also offered more practical solutions. If a World Cup happened to coincide with a summer of exams, you could plan your revision and possibly even your entire strategy around the fixture list. "Right, my Geography GCSE finishes right before the afternoon kick-off for the second group games. Which means if I absolutely nail the section on volcanoes and rock formations, I can get back home in time for the second half of Belgium v Morocco."

They were simpler, happier times.

Whatever the decade, mugs have always been a fertile patch for crap merchandise. Perhaps it's our history as a nation of tea drinkers, but England does seem to have an unquenchable thirst for over-priced, underwhelming china.

One of the great dreams of any true fan is that one day you might meet one of your heroes, and maybe even get to quiz them about the Beautiful Game. Smugs took the latter aspiration one step further. Not only could you pick their brains, you could drink out of them, too.

But first the tricky task of working out which player your Smug was meant to be.

David Seaman... or Magnum PI?

One's a cheery Yorkshireman busy keeping clean sheets, the other a wise-cracking private investigator looking into Hawaii's dirty business. Still, perhaps Tom Selleck could help solve one of football's biggest mysteries: how did a man with the safest hands in the game get lobbed from the halfway line?

Les Ferdinand... or Dave Benson-Phillips?

Les Ferdinand. You remember him. Colossal centre-forward. Leap like a salmon. Newcastle number nine and hero of the Gallowgate End.

At least when he wasn't gleefully dunking parents and teachers into a tank of gunge, much to the delight of a baying mob of small children.

Peter Schmeichel... or East European action-movie villain?

Perhaps the most curious design of all. In fairness, finding an image of Schmeichel when he wasn't barking expletives at Steve Bruce must have been quite the challenge for the manufacturers.

Still, you have to question the decision-making here.

"Let's make him smile and tone down his legendary red hooter that is so often derided by opposition fans."

"Good idea. There's no need to be unkind. to the Danish shotstopper."

"Okay, so while we're at it, let's also give him a psychotic smile and unnecessarily pock-marked skin so he looks like a walking advert for Clearasil."

140

Diving. The scourge of the Beautiful Game. One of our biggest fears when the floodgates opened for foreign stars to pour into English football was that they'd bring some of the dark arts to the bright lights of the Premier League.

We'd seen it in European football and on the international stage, so-called 'clever' forwards conning officials and hitting the deck at the merest hint of contact. We didn't want our impressionable youngsters imitating what they saw on screen in parks and playgrounds across the land.

We wanted them to preserve the honesty of the English game. After all, you wouldn't see young Michael Owen, the nation's great hope, rolling around on the turf when an Argentinian defender sneezed in his direction at the World Cup in a shameless (and successful) attempt to nick a penalty. Absolutely not.

Sadly, on a September afternoon at Hillsborough in 1998, it seemed that it was too late. When English players start play-acting, it's one thing. When the referees are doing it, all is lost.

During the working week, Paul Alcock was the manager of a Kent shopping centre where his main brush with delinquency was stopping gangs of teenagers smoking outside Our Price or gawping at the saucy posters in Athena. At the weekend, he was a top-flight referee, charged with keeping the peace amongst Premier League primadonnas. On this particular Saturday he had quite the job on his hands as Arsenal made the trip to Sheffield Wednesday. It pitched Patrick Vieira against Paolo Di Canio, both men whose tempers made the Incredible Hulk look like a UN diplomat. It didn't take long for the game to reach boiling point.

The irate Italian took exception to Vieira's ample aggression, Martin Keown swung him round by the collar and

chaos ensued. Keown and Di Canio were expelled. Meanwhile Vieira, at the hub of all the aggro, sheepishly whistled 'La Marseillaise' and headed back to midfield.

What happened next was pure Premier League pantomime. Di Canio, owner of the keenest sense of injustice in association football, shoved the referee in disgust – and then Alcock took centre stage. His fall to the floor was pure slapstick, like Charlie Chaplin after six pints and a doner kebab. It was extraordinary viewing, and a wake-up call for the English game. Realistically, we could no longer hold the moral high ground, not when one of our top refs was rolling in the dirt after the sort of contact that wouldn't have toppled Miss Marple.

Afterwards, Wednesday boss Danny Wilson, who had clashed frequently with Di Canio, made no pretence about protecting his Italian superstar. He said the club would happily abide with the FA's punishment, which is a bit like inviting King Herod to your child's christening.

Di Canio copped a £10,000 fine and an eleven-game ban. His time at Wednesday was over. But his – and Alcock's – place in the history books was secure.

141

Baggio is QPR target!

INSANE TRANSFER RUMOURS

Nothing gets a fan's pulse racing quite like a salacious transfer rumour. It doesn't matter how old you are, or how many times you've been hurt before, there's something seductive about seeing a top, top player linked with your club that short-circuits your common sense.

In the '90s, before the internet and social media, transfer gossip was still shrouded in mystery. There was no Google to gather research on exotic names. And there were no ITK (In The Know) sources to ratify the rumours. What you saw was what you got. You were at the mercy of manipulative headline writers who would routinely pull on your heartstrings.

Still, even without the investigatory tools at our disposal, there were some stories that just didn't pass the sniff test. Transfer talk so barely believable that it could only be bollocks... surely?

Roberto Baggio to... QPR?

In the summer of 1995, QPR fans were reeling from the loss of leading scorer Les Ferdinand to Newcastle. Sir Les's goals had been the foundation for three Premier League seasons of top-ten finishes and with only youngsters Kevin Gallen and Danny Dichio left to lead the line, there were concerns at Loftus Road that they needed some experience up front.

So imagine the excitement amongst R's fans when the *Evening Standard* reported that no less a star than World Cup winner Roberto Baggio was potentially on his way to west London. 'The Divine Ponytail' was on his way out of Juventus, and despite rumours linking him to Inter, Manchester United and Real Madrid, Hoops boss Ray Wilkins had apparently stolen a march on his other suitors.

Except he hadn't. Despite Wilkins' charm and his knowledge of Italian football, there was more chance of Baggio picking up the phone to Edward Scissorhands than anyone from Loftus Road. That's not to say that the headline was wrong. Technically, Baggio was indeed of interest – in the same way that as a teenager I was interested in carnal relations with Samantha Fox and Linda Lusardi.

> **Some transfer talk was so barely believable that it could only be bollocks.**

Ultimately, Baggio moved to AC Milan where he would form a deadly partnership with George Weah and win the Scudetto. Meanwhile, Rangers did find the experience they were looking for in the shape of veteran striker Big Mark Hateley. He scored twice. QPR were relegated.

Gabriel Batistuta to... Ipswich Town?

In 1994 Fiorentina superstar Gabriel Batistuta returned from the World Cup with his stock higher than ever before, as Argentina's leading scorer in the USA. However, according to the *Independent*, all was not rosy in Florence.

Apparently Batigol, whose goals had seen La Viola promoted to Serie A, was looking for a new challenge. And, according to reports, he'd already signed a pre-contract agreement elsewhere – meaning his famous partnership with incoming Portuguese star Rui Costa was over before it had even started.

142

His destination? Portman Road. Maybe Batistuta wouldn't miss those moments of Costa magic. After all, he was going to be united with Steve Sedgeley.

It's hard to know precisely what scuppered the deal for the Argentinian. Did he think the language barrier would inhibit his partnership with Boncho Guentchev? Was he afraid of competition for places with Chris Kiwomya? Or was it the fact that the story was a complete and utter fabrication?

Sadly, we never did see that potentially deadly Guentchev-Batistuta axis, and Ipswich fans have spent the last 26 years wondering what might have been. In reality, Town finished rock bottom of the Premier League. And you have to wonder if their forward line was really a priority. Their Player of the Season was keeper Craig Forrest. He conceded 93 goals.

Zinedine Zidane to... Blackburn Rovers?
"Why would we want Zidane? We've got Tim Sherwood."

Of all the things Jack Walker said and did for Blackburn, this was by some distance the worst. No one would ever fault the

chairman's passion for his beloved Rovers, nor the extraordinary generosity that underpinned their 1995 title win. But his decision to turn down one of the greatest players that ever lived would come back to haunt him.

Unlike the rumours above, Zidane's arrival at Ewood Park wasn't the fantasy of a bored journalist sitting over his typewriter struggling to fill his weekly column. The Frenchman had agreed terms on a move alongside fellow countryman Christophe Dugarry – a move which would have been the most exotic thing to happen to Lancashire since they started serving prawn cocktail-flavoured crisps in the Rovers Return.

In the event, Walker overruled Kenny Dalglish's request for the transfer funds to secure the French duo's signatures. Blackburn's title defence was a disaster. Dalglish resigned pre-season, leaving Ray Harford to oversee a seventh-place finish.

Meanwhile, Zidane would go on to win the Champions' League, Serie A, La Liga, the European Championships and, just for good measure, the World Cup. And Tim Sherwood didn't.

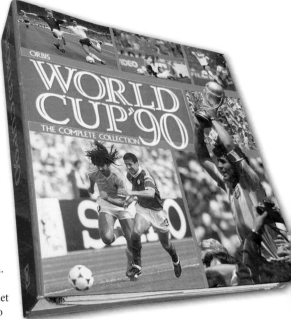

ORBIS: FOOTBALL'S MAGNA CARTA

Think back to famous English documents, and what comes to mind? The *Magna Carta*? Admiral Nelson's battle plan for Trafalgar? The script for the pilot episode of *Minder*? All meritorious in their own right, but for children of a certain generation they are a pale imitation of the real thing: the Orbis World Cup 90 binder and sticker collection.

Advertised on telly by the one and only Brian Clough, this was far more than your average sticker book. It was a treasure trove of knowledge and wisdom. The publication brought to life the rich history of the Jules Rimet Trophy with chapters devoted to great games, iconic goals, and the stars of the upcoming tournament.

It was a scripture of such magnificence that you felt compelled to complete it. By any means necessary.

If the '80s were characterised by the rise of privatisation, stock markets and high-risk boiler-room trades, the '90s began in the same vein. Only this time those frantic negotiations took place not on the trading floors of Wall Street but in school playgrounds. Throughout May and June of 1990 it seemed there was a moratorium on all traditional breaktime activity across the land, as youngsters got down to the business at hand: getting all the weekly magazines and fitting them into the vast ring-binder album, then filling your sticker collection.

There were extraordinary scenes. A microcosm of the ruthless onslaught of capitalism. There was no place for the weak. Negotiations were cut-throat. Transactions processed at breakneck

> **This was far more than your average sticker book. It was a treasure trove of knowledge and wisdom.**

speed. Gordon Gekko told us that 'lunch was for wimps,' and he was right – though an occasional slurp of Um Bongo was positively encouraged.

As common sense gave way to the basic human need for consumption, haste caused hyper-inflation. In my school, the entirety of Italy's defensive line – including Baresi, Maldini and Costacurta – might, just might, get you a sniff of England's Steve Bull.

Go onto eBay and you can still find examples of this work of art, preserved perfectly in plastic shields. It's another reason why, for some of us, that summer of 1990 will never be beaten.

They say that 1992 was the year that football changed forever. Denmark won the European Championships despite not qualifying for the tournament. John Jensen managed a shot on target. Fifa said goodbye to the backpass. And England said hello to the much-feted Premier League, which would soon become the global monolith that it is today.

But for some of us, the most seismic moment of the year happened in the pages of *Amiga Power* with the announcement that Sensible Soccer was coming to a high street near you. It was billed as a revolution in football gaming. And boy, did it deliver.

Players looked like an assortment of little blobs with indiscernible features, which as anyone who's sat in the away end at St James' Park will recognise as an all-too-familiar sensation.

However, much like a scouting report on Diego Maradona, those little blobs with the big hair and stumpy legs were gifted with godlike abilities. What made the game so special was the after-touch part of the gameplay. One twist of the joystick produced the sort of obscene curl and swerve that later made Roberto Carlos a household name.

The best part was that any player, as the Sensi theme music suggested, could be a 'goalscoring superstar hero'. Whether you were Lothar Matthaus or Leo Fortune-West, you could score the sort of ludicrous wonder goals that would give Ferenc Puskas sleepless nights.

Similarly, heading and tackling weren't limited by traditional laws of physics. Players needed only to be within a ten-yard radius to launch themselves into a diving header like Keith Houchen arrowed into the corner in his pomp. Similarly,

> **One twist of the joystick produced the sort of obscene swerve that made Roberto Carlos a household name.**

tackling became something of an art form. There was no such thing as a subtle nudge or cheeky shoulder barge. Violence was positively encouraged. Sensible Soccer felt like a microcosm of Terry Hurlock's career: every challenge was a potential leg-breaker.

With each update, the game's creators

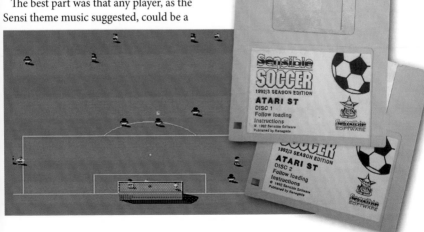

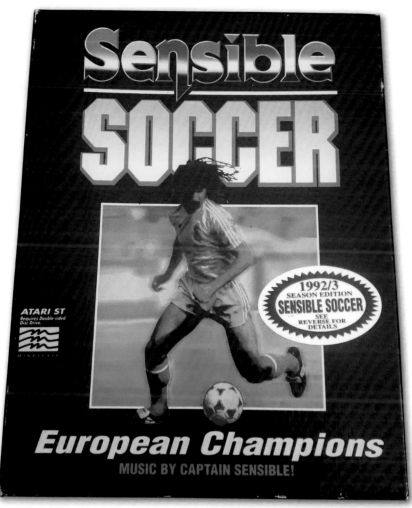

added delightful new wrinkles: huge multi-national databases, league competitions across the globe, player transfers and then, of course, the unrequited joy of the Custom Teams. This was the library of wonderfully nonsensical line-ups. Ever wanted to play as an EastEnders XI and see if that fabled forward line of Ethel and Fat Pat could deliver results at the highest level? This was your chance.

No subject, no matter how mundane or utterly ridiculous, was off-limits.

Cheeseboards – where Stilton and Edam were defensive rocks. Or kebab shop menus – which boasted a tasty attacking trio of small doner, fresh chillies and a cheeseburger – were all part of the irresitible madness.

These days, Sensi may pale somewhat in direct comparison to the lifelike graphics and multi-button machinations of your FIFAs and your Pro Evos. But in terms of sheer unadulterated fun, it's still an all-time classic.

There is now a whole generation of football fans who assume moustaches are only to be grown by hipsters, ironically or as part of some charitable endeavour. But back in the '90s, lip ferrets were the height of masculinity.

On television, Tom Selleck popularised the cookie-duster look via American crime drama *Magnum PI*. In music, Freddie Mercury developed an iconic look that can almost be defined by the nose beard alone. And in the world of sport, Micky Quinn proudly grew some upper-lipped face fungus that marked him out as one of the most unlikely looking footballers in the history of the game.

Sam Allardyce, too, proudly donned bushy lip fur as his playing career tapered down at Preston North End; and, in fact, wore the look so well that even to this day his face looks a little naked without one.

Elsewhere, Scotland and Ipswich defender John Wark blazed a machostache trail with his decision to extend his lip-hamster down in straight lines, on either side of his mouth. My research tells me this particular 'tache style should be known as a 'handlebar moustache' – yet there's something about the unique way that particular snot-mop interplayed with Wark's rugged Scottish features and incredible '90s mullet that almost moves it beyond categorisation. You simply can't put Wark's 'tache in a box.

However, one 'tache that spent a whole career in the box was possibly the best of them all – David Seaman's. You really got the sense with 'Safe Hands' snoz-sweeper, that if you were to pull it off his face and on to a large stick, you'd have yourself an industry-leading broom. As an England fan, there was something quite settling in the '90s about having your national keeper so comfortable with his identity, that he wore a moustache throughout his career.

The world's best at saving shots. And David Seaman.

> **Put it onto a large stick, you'd have yourself an industry-leading broom.**

In fact, if you trace the downfall of Seaman, it came around the same time as his absurd decision to grow a massive ponytail; we can't rule out the possibility that Ronaldinho's lob at the World Cup in 2002 only went in due to the effects of gravity on David Seaman's mass of hair down his back. Fast-forward another four years and Seaman had shaved off the 'tache for *Dancing on Ice* in 2006; the change-of-look curse struck again as Big Dave planted his partner Pam O'Connor firmly down on her face in rehearsals, busting her chin wide open.

Sadly, such tales of footballing facial whiskers are now planted firmly in the past; you'd never see the likes of Raheem Sterling or Jordan Henderson try one out. And as much as I love the '90s, the end of the lip-scarf era might well be welcome news for face-fuzz critics everywhere.

Why not get rid of the old boot,
for something more shapely

MITRE MUNDIAL

This sounds a bit like Henry VIII's online dating profile.

If you were ever lucky enough to be invited to splash some birthday cash at your official club shop, it's almost certain that you went there with the intention of scooping up the big-ticket items; the shirt, maybe a full kit, perhaps even a ball. Having done that, it's likely you might find a spare one or two pounds left over, and that's really the purpose of the cheapest and often most bizarre section in the '90s football retail space: the official club photos.

The West Ham club shop in the '90s (a club shop, lest we forget, that was in fact a static caravan permanently parked in the forecourt behind our main stand) had a series of plexiglass pigeon holes by the till from which you could help yourself to photos of our Claret and Blue stars for a mere 80p a pop. What people did with the photos they collected was up to them; some adorned many a bedroom wall, but a few better-connected types actually managed to get their official photos signed.

And best of all, if you're hankering for a signed photo of your '90s hero, good news. Because the internet is absolutely chock-a-block with them; in fact, you're probably never more than five clicks away from that signed photo of Chris Kiwomya you've always yearned for.

Anyway, to save you the hassle of finding out what's out there in the land of spurious but strangely irresistible collectables, allow me to assist with a rundown of the best and worst signed '90s footballer photos available.

Ian Feuer – West Ham
If you're in need of a signed photo of Ian Feuer – West Ham's substitute goalkeeper, who never made a single appearance for the Hammers in his three-year spell between 1994 and 1996 – then boy, are you going to be glad you bought this book. Because on my 12th birthday in 1995, I found myself at West Ham's static caravan shop, perusing the official photos with a pound left to spend – only to discover that we'd sold out of all of the official player photos, bar one. Yes, that of our unloved and almost universally forgotten back-up keeper, Ian Feuer.

However, this story comes with two bits of bad news. Firstly, as the signed picture

LANCASHIRES PREMIER LEAGUE TEAM
BLACKBURN ROVERS

His chin resting on his hand in a moment of conceited thoughtfulness.

of Ian Feuer is in a box in the loft of my parents' house, it might as well be lodged in some forgotten Pharoah's tomb, and is therefore essentially lost to history. And secondly, the signature is fake because (drum roll) it was I(!) who augmented the official photo with the signature, having duplicated Feuer's autograph from the matchday programme. Yes, I faked Ian Feuer's autograph.

I have literally no idea why I did this other than, I would have to assume, perhaps thinking that one day someone might be impressed by the fact I had met

Ian Feuer; a lie so believable, it's hard to imagine anyone ever questioning it.

So therefore, you won't need a certificate of proof with the signed photo because no one would ever think for one minute that it was fake.

The perfect crime for an imperfect photo of an even more imperfect goalkeeper.

David May – Manchester United

If Ian Feuer doesn't float your boat, there's always the option of investing in this sensational picture of David May; his chin resting on his hand in a moment of conceited thoughtfulness that predates another famous David, in this case Brent, by at least two whole years.

The acquisition of David May by Manchester United made little sense at the time; so what better way to commemorate that transfer than with this equally puzzling pose by the man who led the most famous, undeserved, Champions' League trophy celebration this side of John Terry?

Chris Sutton –
Blackburn Rovers
On what appears to be a boiling hot summer's day, here we see Chris Sutton in a full blazer, best wedding shirt and tie, holding aloft the scarf of his new club while pulling a face that frankly implies that he's had enough of your shit.

Sutton would go on to have a sensational career for Blackburn, netting 47 goals in 130 League games as well as claiming a Premier League title.

In more recent times, however, he's become known as a pundit whose forthright views and serious persona feel a world away from that cheeky chappy who used to smile and hug Ruel Fox after a goalscoring effort. No, these days his demonic nature is far more in line with the evil facials we see here just above his autograph; and what better way to prove you saw the real Sutton coming than by owning this signed snap from 1994?

Brian McClair – Manchester United
The sheer number of bizarre circumstances that have resulted in this

Why has the club photographer elected to seal this moment in immortality with his camera?!

autographed picture being available to purchase are mind-blowing. Firstly, let's take in the scene: here we see Scotland and United striker Brian McClair in an impeccably ironed shirt, while ironing another shirt upon an ironing board decorated with flowers in what we must presume is the Red Devils' laundry hub.

McClair himself sees no humour in the situation, apparently, such is his fixed gaze at the task at hand; ironing. Was this an everyday occurence for the man? And what's more, why has the club photographer elected to seal this moment in immortality with his camera?!

And perhaps the greatest plot twist of all: we have to ask why someone has then presented McClair with this picture of him ironing to sign?

And then why has someone else decided it has monetary value in an online auction?

For insurance purposes, Ian Feuer was 80p in 1995; Julian Joachim just £2.75, last week.

A truly absurd set of circumstances that I doubt we'll ever satisfactorily get to the bottom of.

Julian Joachim – Aston Villa

One immediate thing to note on this image of Aston Villa's small yet occasionally supersonic striker is the scrawl that we are to assume is Julian Joachim's autograph.

Call me old fashioned, but I've long thought that autographs should at least bear a passing resemblance

to the name they are supposed to represent. And having double-checked just now, I can still confirm that Julian Joachim's name is in fact Julian Joachim and not 'luuuuu luuuuu'.

But nevertheless, a lovely gift for someone crying out for a graffitied picture of an oft-injured '90s footballer.

Finally, the bit for collectors and dealers, like on *Bargain Hunt*. For insurance purposes, Ian Feuer cost 80p in 1995; just last week, Julian was a very reasonable £2.75, David May only cost £3.00, Sutton £3.50 and McClair £3.75, making him the winner. Well done, Choccy.

Anyone who has ever kicked a ball around a garden or local park will know of the one element that can transform a kickabout into a truly special game of football; nets. The swoosh, hitting one into the roof, clipping one into the side, the sight of a downtrodden goalkeeper bending over to scoop one out of the very back; sights and sounds that are infinitely better than pounding a shot through a netless goal, then watching it roll silently into the distance, or worse still flying into a bush or neighbour's garden.

The '90s were a fantastic era for the goal net, and some remain more memorable than others. For example, **Portman Road, Ipswich Town, 1993**...

These were nets as inexplicably deep as they were inexplicably designed. Being something of a '90s goal stanchion aficionado, I have seen just about every make and model, every iteration of design to give the net some structure as it moves away from the goal line. However, in the long history of football, never again were we to see the type of experimentation that occurred in Suffolk in 1993.

Firstly, they had those curved pieces of metal from the top of the post down. The same construction that effectively caught the ball for Sir Trevor Brooking's sensational goal for England away to Hungary in 1981. So far, so what? But then we get to the stanchions. Where to start? Well, they're too small for one, they're also pitifully shallow. The net hangs around all of this like a festival tent put up by a drunkard. Then there's the actual net itself; it extends on the ground for another half a metre beyond these measly, mini-stanchions. The end result of all this is the first post-modern goal frame of the Premier League era. It's a mess of ideas; a nightmare of a goal fixture.

Then there's **The Dell, Southampton, 1992**. If these nets were before your time, I'm not sure I can adequately describe how inadequate they were for top-level football. The nets were about half a metre deep. Beyond that, flush to to the net, a pair of stanchions kept them taut; and finally, flush to the stanchions, was an advertising board with a row of children's faces resting upon it. All of these items, from the touchline to the first fan, were all comfortably within a metre or so.

One of the sights I've missed most since the '90s is undoubtedly youngsters' faces pressed into the back of the net; so close that if a powerful shot went in, there was little any net could do to prevent some red-faced child screaming their way home for an early bath. As football has moved on and stadiums been redesigned, so too have we bid farewell to 'minimum nettage' like those at The Dell, but not before their finest moment...

11th August 1999, Southampton v Leeds. The Saints trail 1-0 to a Michael Bridges goal (remember him?), when from a corner Mark Hughes thumps a thunderous volley (remember how good he was at them?) into the goal with such ferocity, that it cannons back off the advertising hoarding and back into play in the blink of an eye.

Astonishingly, despite the crowd behind that shallow net rightfully celebrating a goal, no one on the Southampton team has an inkling that it might have gone in, so Leeds hook the ball away and referee Alan Wiley doesn't acknowledge the goal. An astonishing cameo from one of the great and yet most useless nets of the '90s.

And how can we forget **Stamford Bridge, Chelsea, 1993?** Stamford Bridge was a mad old place in the '90s. There was electric fencing and chicken wire keeping fans from the pitch. I remember going there and sitting upon cold, hard concrete in a stand that arched its way round the pitch at an angle more suited to greyhound racing. But possibly most bizarre of all,

Goals were made all the better at USA 94 courtesy of those amazing goal nets.

there were the cars parked behind the goal for purposes that I always assumed lay somewhere between advertising and being an actual working car park.

And so it fell upon the goal frame and nets to provide some normality to proceedings. What we got instead was a set of goals that closely mimicked those of a Subbuteo set. There are bars protruding from every imaginable angle, leaving onlookers with the absolute certainty that this robust frame would survive a nuclear war, or even worse, a Mark Hughes volley.

But ultimately, the best goal nets of the '90s undoubtedly belonged to **World Cup USA 94**. I know it's a controversial favourite. Call me out of touch and old-fashioned, but I do like a classic, deep, thick-stringed, white net.

The only debate left after that, which has raged for centuries and torn families apart, is the classic late-night pub debate: 'Where do you stand on stanchions?' I can almost hear the collective sigh as I begin to offer an opinion on this fractious matter.

Call me a heretic, but the goal nets of USA 94 achieved something that even now seems impossible; they were innovative, amazing, iconic and never really repeated since. The design was remarkable, with two long poles sticking out behind the goal

to offer the net a wonderfully floaty yet structured appearance.

Actual goals were made all the better at that World Cup courtesy of those amazing goal nets. Seeing a ball strike the corner of the goal and then curl round the net; or a long-range effort flexing the American meshwork to its maximum extent remains an incredibly satisfying sight.

Gheorghe Hagi's effort straight into the top bin against Colombia. Klinsmann's acrobatic masterpiece against South Korea. Maradona's spectacular work against Greece. All these iconic moments were elevated by the goal nets they were scored in. All sensational, but the reality is no one really remembers. Because none was as iconic as Diana Ross's penalty miss in the opening ceremony.

The launch of the Premier League in 1992 was full of surprises. There was the kaleidoscopic horror of Richard Keys' wardrobe, the high kicks and pom-poms of Sky's cheerleaders. And then, when the football started, there was the inexplicable rise of Norwich City.

During the '80s, the Canaries had tootled along nicely in the top tier of English football. They always stayed up, never went down, and spent most of the time camped around the top half – which sounds like an extract from Hugh Hefner's memoirs.

In 1991/92 they completely collapsed, having finished just above the relegation zone the previous season after a calamitous run of nine defeats in the last eleven games. Manager Dave Stringer was sacked and replaced by reserve-team boss Mike Walker, or 'Mr Nobody', as most of the football world referred to him.

After selling star striker Robert Fleck to Chelsea and then replacing him with Manchester United reserve Mark Robins – who hadn't scored a single League goal the previous season – Norwich were immediately installed as hot favourites for the drop.

To everyone's surprise, not least their

> ❝ *Mike Walker's side became everyone's favourite underdogs as neutral fans cheered on their unlikely title tilt.* ❞

own, they won 4-2 at title contenders Arsenal on the inaugural day of Premier League activity. Robins, who had hair like Vera Duckworth's stunt double, notched twice and the Canaries were flying high. Incredibly, they soared to new heights by putting together an extraordinary run of form which saw them at the top of the

table for long stretches of the season.

Their high-tempo, attacking football attracted much praise from the press and the punters. Soon Mike Walker's side became everyone's favourite underdogs as neutral fans cheered on their unlikely title tilt. It must have been galling for Sky, who'd built their marketing machine for

the new League on glitz and glamour. Yet here it was being topped by a ragtag bunch of journeymen.

There were no stars at Carrow Road. Just good, honest professionals. The defence was marshalled by two Ians (Culverhouse and Butterworth), both of whom looked like they worked at a local chartered accountancy. In midfield they had the perfect mix of spit and sawdust, as playmaker Ian Crook gelled nicely with the honest endeavour of Jeremy Goss, a man who could have walked into his own living room without being recognised. And in attack little Ruel Fox, quicker than a sausage down a water slide, proved a

157

potent addition to the upfront pairing of Robins and Chris Sutton.

They were brave and breathtaking in equal measure. The likes of Villa, Chelsea, Leeds and Liverpool were humbled as City kept pace with the leaders into springtime.

Ultimately, they faded towards the finish line, securing third place in the table as Eric Cantona inspired Manchester United to top spot. However, their heroics were rewarded with a place in the UEFA Cup, and City would begin their own European adventure the following campaign.

On a magnificent night in Munich, Jeremy Goss volleyed home one of the goals of the decade to secure a sensational win.

Their enthusiasm wasn't necessarily shared by the pundits. Norwich's late-season wobble was construed as the early onset of the dreaded Second Season Syndrome (they would ultimately finish a disappointing 12th in 1993/94), and most expected their journey to the continent to yield the same sort of success as that of a seasick Viking.

Despite patchy League form, the Canaries relished their UEFA Cup

sojourn. Efan Ekoku, whose hitherto claim to fame was that you could whistle his name perfectly to the tune of the Linda McCartney jingle, scored their first ever goal in European competition in the first-round rout of Vitesse Arnhem.

They were rewarded with a trip to the mighty Bayern. And on a magnificent night in Munich, Jeremy Goss volleyed home one of the goals of the decade to secure a sensational win that made Mike Walker's men the most successful East Anglian export since Delia Smith's recipe for roasted parsnips.

Eventually, it took some serious brilliance from Inter's Dennis Bergkamp to bring their odyssey to an end.

Today that Canaries side, in their distinctive scrambled-egg-and-cress shirts, is remembered and rightly feted by nostalgic Norfolkers and neutrals alike. Manchester United may have won the silverware, but it was Norwich City who won our hearts.

"Someone get the magic sponge…"

When Jurgen Klinsmann signed for Spurs from Monaco in the summer of 1994, it sent shockwaves through English football. Not only was one of the best strikers on the entire planet coming to the Premier League, but he was going to play in the same team as Jason Dozzell. It felt like a Championship Manager fever dream.

Once the dust settled, there were some question marks about how he'd settle in his new home. And not all were pleased to see him. In an era when English fans saw more of *Button Moon* than they did European club football, the striker had earned a reputation based on his international appearances. And though the blonde bombshell's goals had powered the German side to glory at Italia 90, it was also a tournament where he spent more time horizontal than Hugh Hefner on his birthday.

His arrival was greeted with red-top headlines such as 'Dive Bomber' – straight out of the Basil Fawlty School of Journalism – a jibe which Klinsmann laughed off admirably by casually asking, "Are there any diving schools nearby?" at his unveiling in front of the massed ranks of the world's media.

In hindsight, quite how such a global talent was lured to White Hart Lane remains nothing short of miraculous. A deal was agreed on Alan Sugar's yacht – conveniently moored in the harbour of Monte Carlo – a salubrious surrounding that masked the mayhem the Spurs chairman was dealing with back home.

Even for a club whose finger hovers perennially over the self-destruct button, these were desperate times at Tottenham Hotspur. The ruling of a long-running FA investigation into illegal player payments under the previous ownership had landed Spurs a whopping £600,000 fine,

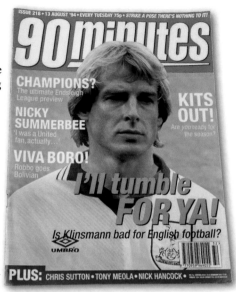

ISSUE 218 • 13 AUGUST '94 • EVERY TUESDAY 75p • STRIKE A POSE THERE'S NOTHING TO IT!

90 minutes

CHAMPIONS?
The ultimate Endsleigh
League preview

KITS OUT!
Are you ready for
the season?

NICKY SUMMERBEE
I was a United
fan, actually...

VIVA BORO!
Robbo goes
Bolivian

I'll tumble FOR YA!
Is Klinsmann bad for English football?

UMBRO

PLUS: CHRIS SUTTON • TONY MEOLA • NICK HANCOCK •

a 12-point penalty, and they were banned from the FA Cup into the bargain.

Still, the lure of London and a new adventure was too much for Klinsmann to ignore, despite the administrative chaos he was walking into. On the pitch, any pretence that Spurs were at the forefront of football's tactical revolution soon dissipated. On a pre-season tour to Dublin,

> **At Italia 90, he spent more time horizontal than Hugh Hefner on his birthday.**

Ossie Ardiles bowled into the dressing room, handed every player 30 quid and told them to pop down the boozer. *Welcome to English football, Jurgen. Pint of Stella please, mate.*

In fairness, Klinsmann enjoyed the *joie de vivre* of his new manager in comparison to the discipline of his continental counterparts. It's hard to know what they were doing in the sprawling training complexes of Inter or AS Monaco, but it's safe to assume they weren't tucking into pints and packets of Frazzles.

When the season proper was underway, Ardiles displayed all the tactical discipline of a World War II kamikaze pilot. Spurs debuted the season with the lesser-spotted 3-2-5 formation in a pulsating opening day performance at Hillsborough, where Klinsmann scored the winner in a 4-3 win and celebrated with a full-length dive into the turf that poked fun at his reputation.

This was the madcap blueprint for the Ardiles era. The press christened Klinsmann, Teddy Sheringham, Darren Anderton, Ilie Dumitrescu and Nick Barmby 'The Famous Five', in tribute to the romantic nature of this free-flowing football philosophy. But, sadly, you don't win Premier League games with fanciful fairytales. And besides, even Enid F**king Blyton knows that someone has to put their foot in.

Predictably, Spurs conceded goals – and games – thick and fast, and Sugar's patience wore thin. A chastening League Cup defeat at Notts County meant that Ossie wasn't going to Wembley; he was off to the Jobcentre

instead. His replacement was the very picture of consistency – Gerry Francis – a man who had unashamedly kept the same hairstyle since 1972.

The change of manager, and outlook, did little to affect the German striker's form. Klinsmann remained absolutely lethal in front of goal, notching 29 goals in 50 appearances and earning himself the Football Writers' Association Player of the Year award. He had changed the face of the Premier League, throwing open the gates for an influx of high-profile foreign stars such as Dennis Bergkamp, Ruud Gullit and Juninho.

When he left in the summer to return to his homeland (signing for Bayern Munich), it felt like the end of a whirlwind romance. His humility and charm – he was frequently pictured driving around London in his VW Beetle – had won him a legion of new fans across the land. He'd swept English football off its feet. And stayed on his.

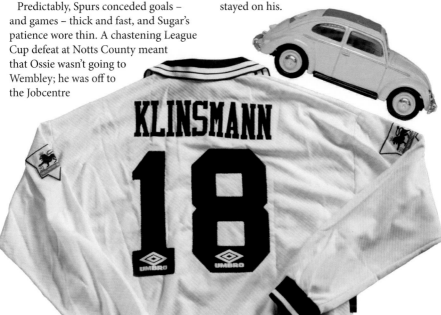

At the very start of the '90s, football clubs didn't quite have 'merchandise catalogues', they were a tad more akin to 'merchandise pamphlets'. No brainiac had yet figured out that you could apply a club crest to just about anything and flog it. However, by the end of the decade, club catalogues were longer than Roberto Baggio's ponytail and jam-packed full of a cacophony of crap that even Del Boy might've refused to peddle.

The traditional '90s club catalogue started with the old standards: club kits. Usually your best player in the home kit, displaying it in all its glory while doing a few kick-ups. Then your second-best player in the away kit, perhaps leaning on a post with a ball under his arm. And finally the goalkeeper, leaping to catch a ball in a manner that was patently staged. Of course, in the '90s, these kits would've been worn two years at a time, representing something like decent value

for the owner. Nowadays, kits seem to have all the longevity of Ali Dia's Southampton spell. But alas, we're here to talk about the rubbish in club catalogues and, after kits, things start getting a little spicy.

Loungewear and leisure wear is where things would really start kicking off. No club catalogue is complete without the sight of one of your '90s heroes looking visibly uncomfortable while rocking a naff shirt that no one in their right mind would ever dream of owning.

From here, things escalate: swimwear, babywear, lunchboxes, mouse mats and stuffed toys. Little kits to hang in the back window of your car. Mints, jelly beans and chocolate bars. A little replica of the stadium to adorn your desk with. Pin badges, little cassettes of questionable musical value, books and branded club bookmarks.

Then there were merchandise collaborations that boggled the mind: from a tube of Pritt Stick with your club's badge

The most idyllic scene to be found in the catalogue was always the boudoir shot.

on it to Pez dispensers with (you guessed it) your club's badge on it.

But the most idyllic scene to be found in the entire catalogue was almost always the boudoir shot. An image that seemed to answer the question, "What would happen if my football team's crest threw up over my childhood bedroom." You'd have bedspreads, pillowcases, clocks, wallpaper, doormats and lampshades; through a child's eyes, this particular vista represented the new gold standard of football fandom.

Because here's the thing about being a football-obsessive child in the '90s: you literally did want your club crest plastered over any old rubbish. From pencil cases to slippers, no Christmas list was complete without a couple of items lifted from your club's half-baked, mercilessly commercialised merchandise catalogue. Money-making scheme? Yes. But do we '90s football fans, to this day, still scour eBay for some of these items? Also, yes.

If you'd have been on the side of the M602 in Eccles, Greater Manchester on the 26th February 1999, it's likely you would have seen a BMW get pulled up by the police for illegally driving up the hard shoulder to avoid traffic. When the police pulled that car over, they no doubt would have been astounded to be met by the presence of Sir Alex Ferguson in the driving seat.

The officers dealt with Sir Alex, who made no mention of the defence he would later rely on in court, handed him his ticket and sent him on his way. Fast-forward a few months, however, and Fergie was in court to appeal the charge of illegally driving on a motorway hard shoulder. His defence was astonishing, but quite incredibly, also successful: he claimed he had been on the verge of soiling himself at the time.

Yes. Manchester United's greatest-ever manager gave evidence in Bury Magistrates' Court to the effect that he'd been suffering from severe diarrhoea at the time and was rushing back, up the hard shoulder, to Old Trafford to use the facilities. He further shared that he hadn't mentioned this to the police officers present at the time out of sheer embarrassment at his predicament.

As he testified in court: "When I got into the snarl-up of traffic I took another Imodium tablet. I stayed there for about four or five minutes. I then decided to try and get back to Old Trafford."

His solicitor Nick Freeman (who would later become a celebrity road-traffic lawyer known by the nickname 'Mr Loophole'), asked: "Putting it bluntly, did you need to go to the toilet?" Sir Alex replied: "That was very much the case. I had to go somewhere quickly."

Mr Loophole went on to explain that his client had two options that day: "One is unthinkable and one is to take evasive action". Suffice to say, Sir Alex went for the option that didn't involve shitting himself and successfully argued his way out of a few points on the licence.

Elsewhere in '90s faecal folklore, there's a serious case for suggesting Gerry Francis's reign as Spurs manager came a cropper on account of a crapper. 4th October 1997, and Gerry's ailing Tottenham team

Fergie's solicitor would later become a celebrity road-traffic lawyer known by the nickname 'Mr Loophole'.

come to St James' Park in desperate need of some points in their early-season relegation battle. Gerry must've thought his luck was out when key defender John Scales got injured while running on to the pitch to line up for kick-off.

But things got even more strange after half-time, as Newcastle kicked off the second half against a Spurs team with two players missing. The rumour on Tyneside is that someone had spotted that ex-Toon heroes Ruel Fox and 'Sir' Les

Ferdinand had popped into the bogs and, seeking revenge for their transfer to Spurs, promptly decided to lock them in!

Presumably after some cries for help, our dynamic poo-oh were released by an

Gerry Francis's reign as Spurs manager came a cropper on account of a crapper.

innocent bystander. But even to this day, Ruel and Sir Les refuse to engage with the subject – adding a certain air of mystery to what one must assume was already an air of doo-doo.

The game finished 1-0 to Newcastle and, less than a month later, Gerry Francis was out of a job.

But it wasn't just footballer dung stealing the headlines in the '90s either, there was plenty of player pee-pee to be found, too. The original and best Ronaldo found

himself at the 1996 Olympics in Atlanta. Brazil had lost their opening group game in a shock 1-0 defeat to Japan. Up next, R9 was up against against Hungary.

Brazil took the lead, then Hungary equalised; the Hungarians celebrated and Ronaldo knew he had to do something drastic. El Fenomeno grabbed the ball to hide his modesty, squatted down, and proceeded to take a leak right there in the middle of the pitch.

With the intoxicating smell of urine dampening the will of the Hungary team, Brazil then staged a remarkable comeback to win the game 3-1. From here, Ronaldo rocketed through the tournament until a shock extra-time golden goal in the semi-finals from Nigeria's Nwanko Kanu dumped Brazil out of a gold-medal match via a 4-3 defeat.

Ronaldo scored in the bronze-medal match as Brazil smashed Portugal 5-0. So, in many respects, R9 expertly deployed his bladder to win bronze.

The inferior cousin to footballer coins, Pogs and just about any form of rendered plastic in the history of humankind, Wotsits Whooshers were a special kind of '90s football crap. This was ostensibly a game, but I'm fairly sure no one ever knew the rules. As the name implied, I suppose the idea was you 'whooshed' them hither and tither; but most of the time they were 'whooshed' straight into the bin or occasionally at someone's head on the school bus.

There were two types of Wotsits Whoosher; you either had a tightly cropped, cardboard cut-out of a '90s football star atop some plastic or, most hilariously, '90s football faces fabricated in plastic form, very much in the style of the cryogenically frozen carcass of Hans Solo in *The Empire Strikes Back*.

Crisps in the '90s were far more of a faff than they are today. There was a period when 'Salt and Shake' was the proverbial flavour of the month, mainly on account of the novelty that came with having to locate and rip

> **Very much in the style of the cryogenically frozen carcass of Hans Solo in *The Empire Strikes Back*.**

166

open the salt sachet inside the crisps, before manually salting them yourself. Very much in the same spirit, Wotsits Whooshers also involved having to remember to delve around inside your packet to pull out the elusive whoosher, lest you should accidentally devour a tasteless effigy of Paul Parker.

Obviously, the little plastic people looked nothing like the real thing; David Seaman looked like the policeman from 'Allo 'Allo. Gareth Southgate had a chin so pointy, you could pop a balloon with the end of it. Graeme Le Saux looked like a wartime child who'd just been told he was evacuating to the countryside. Paul Scholes resembled a member of Enid Blyton's Fabulous Four. And Ryan Giggs looked like an electrocuted Hyacinth Bucket from *Keeping Up Appearances*.

There are few professions more precarious than that of football manager. These days, it carries the same job security as deckchair attendant on the *Titanic*. But in the '90s, without the pressure of social media and fan channels, clubs would allow managers a little more grace at the helm – though ultimately you were still at the whim of your chairman and his word, which often meant precisely nothing. There were many gaffers who received the dreaded vote of confidence, only to find themselves gifted with a P45 days later. That was the game, unfortunately.

Unless, of course, you were Mark McGhee. Although the Scot wore the permanent visage of a man who'd just been issued with a parking ticket, in the mid '90s he was a young managerial talent tipped for the top flight. So when Premier League Leicester City approached Reading

about McGhee taking their managerial vacancy, Royals supremo John Madejski went into a full-on charm offensive.

After plying his prized asset with fine wine, Madejski toasted McGhee's decision to remain at Elm Park with a bottle of champagne and telephoned the local paper to tell them the good news. The bubble burst the next morning when he discovered McGhee and his agent were already in Leicester signing paperwork. Madejski was shocked. The last people to get up that early to go to the Midlands were the Luftwaffe.

McGhee had successfully won a game that was rigged against him. And 12 months later he did it again. With his stock riding high at Leicester, he cashed in and joined Wolves. Foxes fans were understandably stunned, though the real victim of this was the club cartoonist – having already finished that year's Christmas card, he had to hastily replace McGhee with a festive Steve Walsh.

As Martin O'Neill led the club to a period of unprecedented success, Leicester fans' anger at McGhee (who was sacked by Wolves in 1998) subsided. He wasn't quite forgiven, however, and when O'Neill led the club into Europe, thousands of postcards were handed out among supporters in Madrid.

They were pre-addressed to Mark McGhee at Molineux and carried the simple message, 'Wish you were here?'

AD NAUSEAM

No11

Reebok rightly received plenty of plaudits for these adverts focussing on alternate timelines, with Dennis Bergkamp making cheese, Ryan Giggs selling flowers, Peter Schmeichel farming pigs and Andy Cole working in a chippy.

Apparently, there was another version where Stephane Guivarc'h posed as a Premier League striker, but that was considered too far-fetched.

AUTHORS

Chris Scull and Sid Lambert have joined forces to create the ultimate celebration of '90s football. Chris is the co-host and co-creator of the smash hit '90s football podcast *Quickly Kevin, will he score?* which was selected as one of *The Observer*'s podcasts of the year in 2017 and won bronze at the 2018 British Podcast Awards. Sid Lambert is a viral sensation, running his hugely popular nostalgic football Twitter account It's A Funny Old Game. His work on the good, the great and the utterly appalling of '90s football has featured in *Planet Football*, *Mundial* and the West Ham United matchday programme.

PICTURE CREDITS

Simon Smith – simonsmithillustrator.co.uk: Dia 10; Souness 11; Rijkaard & Voller 22; Five Bellies & Gazza 35; Atkinson & umbrella 41; O'Neill 54; McGregor 67; Big Jack & The Pope 78; Barbados v Grenada 97.
David Morcom Photography: Cantona and Vinnie cover; Cantona 2; Vialli 7; Moncur 21; Razor 29; Leicester 32; Izzet & Cottee 40; Petit 42; Keegan 50, 51; Atkinson 52, 53; Gullit 57; Vinnie 58, 59; Dublin 69; Fergie 85; Crowd 93; Ginola 102; Bully 134; Cantona 136; McGhee 168; Emerson 174; O'Neill and Keegan back cover.
WellOffside.com: Taylor cover; Wright 9; Holland-England 18; Lineker 24; Ginola 103; Norwich-Bayern 156.
Dave Price: Forest cover; Villa cover; Arsenal 2; Newcastle 174.
Paddy @90sfootball: Shearer Corinthian cover; Dicks Corinthian 3; Baggio Corinthian 42; Shearer & Sutton 74; Jones 122; Souness 123; Pearce 124; Keane 125.
Hinson Chung @thepredatorpro on Instagram: Predator cover; Predators 120, 121.
Martin Thomas: Neville statuette 30.
John Silke: Beckham 86.
Stephen Mather: Blackpool season ticket 92.

ACKNOWLEDGEMENTS

Chris: "For Sophie and Isobel; who, quite rightly, will be baffled by the contents of this book."

Sid: "To Emma, Poppy and Ruby, who have no interest in the subject matter of this book whatsoever. One day I'll regale you all with tales of Ceefax, Sensible Soccer, and Alan Cork's beard."

Thanks to Michael Marden for penning our foreword.
Rob Stokes: thanks for sourcing the elusive Dani cover, page 81.
Neville Evans & Simon 'Shakey' Shakeshaft: thanks for letting us come and photograph bits of the fantastic National Football Collection/National Football Shirt Collection 161.
Dan Farrimond, Alistair Buxton and Jason Robertson, for their help in retrieving the Teletext imagery.

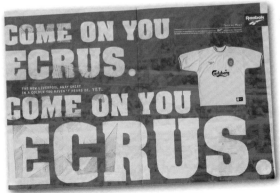

TEAMWORK

Grateful thanks to everyone who subscribed in advance to *Can We Not Knock It?*

Gareth Davis | Tim Seely | Elliott Kerr | Joe Playle | Jack Pryar

Andy Haywood | Danny Sohal | Simon Mearns | Tom Gent

Sam Durant | James Brooker | Andrew Collon | Tom Spinks

Alan Carroll | Björn Berg Gunnarsson | Andrew Wilcock

Jonny Henderson | Daniel & Kim Burdett | Nick Jenkinson

Peter Rednall | Richard Stone | Dan O'Grady | Daniel Thompson

Anthony Hall | Matt Crabb | Anthony Ash | Sam Sandiford

Danny Carr | Steve Greenwood | Gareth Canvin | John Chadwick

Deke Hardman | Ant Coombes | Colin Peppiatt | Nick Piggott

Michael Bray | Jordan Barker | Max Owen | Dylan Ellis

Oliver Gaudion | Tony Stephenson | Dan Townshend | Allan Scott

Stuart York | Dave Clayton | James Ealey | Bradley Barber

Dominic Collier | Stu's Football Flashbacks | Jon Bounds | Paul Clark

Pete Wynne | Andreas Dittmann-Monsen | Jared Driskill | Jon Perks

Alex Rourke | Jacob Stephenson | James Jordan | Duncan Sagar

Dominik Godfrey | Steve James | Malcolm James | D Daly

Beth & Daniel Taylor | Chris Springett | Glenn Johnson | Aaron Sagar

Ian Robert Williamson | Joe Collins | Ben Davies | Greig Saddington

David Fleming | Gavin Warhurst | Lloyd White | Phil Moody

Antony Angeli | David Thackray | Russell Harper | Michael Squires

Robi Thwaites | Mike Brandon | Adam 'Double Doors' Doughty

Chris Regan | Phil Regan | Peter Regan | Simon Baker

Alistair Eddleston | Damian Mawdsley | Anthony Ferguson

Susan Slack | Luke Marchant | Rob Davenport | Lloyd Starr

David Wixon | Mark Ibbetson | Gareth Hunt | Tom Mills

Dan Maxwell | Chris Payne | Peter Baldwin | Andrew Collier

Thomas Rogers | Stuart Chadwick | Chris Oakes | Michael Wheeler

Sam Lewis | Alan Walsh | Dave Clare | Matthew Symes | Ian Rockliffe

Simon Mitchell | Adam Miller | Sam Lawrence | Samantha Hikmet

Neil Boughton | Matt Guest | Mark O'Meara | James Andrew

Shaky Kearney XJ8 | Richard Drew | Ed Townend | Dave Stevens

Richard Stead | Martin Dean | Stu Fanson | Paul Johnston

Tim Carvell | Nick John | James Jackson | Rich Jarvis | Scott Leger

Andy Marciniak | William Kirkham | David London | Gary Brown

Ben Aynsley | Zach Hubbersty | Steven Bostock | Alan Wilson

Graham Dobson | Ainsley Knights | Tom Howard | Adam Hartles

Rob Browne | Matt Braddock | Karen Lee-Kong | Tom Good

Max Camplin | Martin Kay | Derek Taylor | Dave Mathieson

Matthew Clayton | Nigel Westall | Graham Brooke | Max Bull

Greg Braniff | Gary Hegarty | Nicholas Jackson | Russell Finer

Andrew Stean | Alex Kalorkoti | Richard Abberley | Steven Allen

Zane Spelman | Michael Checkley | Stephanie Keenan | Matt Joiner

Matthew Jones | John Turnbull | Andrew Wilson | Helen Longworth

Phil Spencer | Dan Farrimond | Stephen Gutteridge | Mark Terris

Simon Wells | Wayne Salim | Matt Hunter

Kieron Shiel | Thomas Newton

Paul Meek | Matthew Taylor | Helen Emmett

Stuart Power | Sam Hollingsworth

Simon Bailey | Jonnie Dance

Fraser Szymborski-Welsh | James Cockerill

Thomas Kirkland | David Smith

Ross Matthews | William Carter

Matt Brown | Roger Milburn

Nicola Regan | Adrian Harrop